FOCUS

FOCUS

A Collection of Devotions

Seeing Christ in Everything

Tom Sperry

EQUIP PRESS

Colorado Springs

FOCUS

Copyright © 2021 Tom Sperry

All rights reserved. No part of this publication may be reproduced, distributed, or transmitted in any form or by any means, without prior written permission.

Published by Equip Press, Colorado Springs, CO

Unauthorized reproduction of this publication is prohibited. Used by permission. All rights reserved.

Scripture quotations marked (NIV) are taken from the Holy Bible, New International Version. Copyright © 1973, 1978, 1984, 2011 by Biblica, Inc.® Used by permission. All rights reserved worldwide.

Scriptures quotations taken from The Jerusalem Bible copyright © 1966 by Darton, Longman & Todd, Ltd.

First Edition: 2021
Focus / Tom Sperry
Paperback ISBN: 978-1-951304-78-2
eBook ISBN: 978-1-951304-79-9
Library of Congress Control Number: 2021918173

EQUIP PRESS
Colorado Springs

Dedicated to my wonderful wife Debbi,
My children Jennifer and Douglas,
And my grandsons Jackson, Austin, Mason, and Tyler

In a time filled with distractions, we need to keep our focus on Christ more than ever. He is our hope and peace in a world of turmoil. He is our joy and comfort in our times of need. In every situation, He is present. Focus on Him.

I have written these devotions over the past twenty years with the hope that they might encourage the reader. The thoughts are my own and are not meant to represent any particular denomination or dogma. All biblical references are from The Jerusalem Bible unless noted. I have found this translation to be very readable and easy to understand. I have substituted the word God for Yahseh as a personal preference.

I am a retired pharmacist, having practiced pharmacy for thirty-eight years with a BS degree in pharmacy from the University of the Pacific. In 2018, I earned a bachelor of theology degree from Northwestern Theological Seminary and have been involved in developing a school chaplaincy program for elementary-age children. Writing these devotions has helped me with my faith, and I pray that the reader may find some devotions that are helpful and an encouragement.

RECOGNIZE HIS WILL

*"And do not be thoughtless, but recognize
what is the will of the Lord."*

EPHESIANS 5:17

How aware are you of the will of the Lord? Are your actions the result of the awareness of the will of the Lord, or merely thoughtless reactions? The actions of Christians are to be ones of responsibility, understanding, and awareness.

The motives of a Christian should represent the will of the Lord. This requires active thinking, active perceptions, active living, and the willingness to actively seek Christ in everything. It is easy to be thoughtless when God is not at the center of our existence. It is much easier to go through life reacting to situations, putting only the needs of ourselves first.

This verse tells us that we are to live lives of recognition. This requires a willingness to be open in all situations and be sensitive to the will of the Lord. This means we must listen with our heads and hearts. We must commit to thinking before acting and be willing to contemplate situations with the guidance of God's principles before we merely react. It requires the use of our hearts and minds together to shape our actions to obtain a result that is pleasing to God.

One thing that we must have to recognize the will of the Lord is a personal and intimate relationship with Him. Our hearts must be a place where the Holy Spirit dwells, creating the necessary environment for understanding and obedience. We do not make our circumstances, but we do have the ability to react to circumstances as the Lord would have us do when we allow our lives to be directed by God's will, not our own. Recognition of God's will is not always as easy as it may sound. Recognition requires openness, humility, awareness, and discipline. Recognition is a word that demands action and commitment. Think before you act. Use your actions in all circumstances to reflect the will of the Lord.

> *"Where there is no vision the people get out of hand;*
> *blessed are they that keep the Precept."*
>
> **PROVERBS 29:18**

BE HUMBLE

"Though I am free and belong to no man, I make myself a slave to everyone, to win as many as possible."

1 CORINTHIANS 9:19

Are you humble? How important do you think you are? God created us as free men and women, capable of choosing right from wrong, and equally capable of establishing our own importance. How will you use this freedom today? Will you spend the day meeting your own needs, or finding ways to meet the needs of others?

In this verse Paul calls himself a slave to everyone. He has humbled himself and has committed himself to win as many souls as possible. Take time today to consider the souls of the people you come into contact with. Are you actively trying to win them? Are you willing to give up some of your liberties to become their slaves? Paul sacrificed much in order to bring as many people as possible to know Christ. He invested in their lives.

How many of us take the time to show empathy and compassion to those around us? How many of us are willing to sacrifice a part of ourselves in order to elevate others? This is sometimes a difficult task, one that requires a humble attitude. Today make an effort to put others first. Consider the feelings of others toward your actions. Find the needs of others and make yourself a slave to them to meet those needs. We have a great capacity to help others. Consider the sacrifice of Christ on the cross for our benefit. Dedicate yourself to winning as many as possible.

"The reward of humility is the fear of God, riches, honor and life."

PROVERBS 22:4

SET YOUR HEART

"Set your hearts on His kingdom first, and on His righteousness, and all these things will be given to you as well."

MATTHEW 6:33

So many things compete for our attention and efforts. So many things compete for primary importance in our lives and demand our focus. Where does God fit in? How much importance do we ascribe to God? Is He the primary focus in your life?

This verse makes very clear that God should take the pole position in our lives! It tells us to set our hearts and our deepest feelings on His kingdom. Our heart determines our attitudes and priorities. It determines true importance in our lives and gives our existence meaning and depth. Our heart reveals the real truth about ourselves.

Too often our heart is not committed. This verse says "set" your heart on His kingdom, firmly attaching it to His kingdom and righteousness. Our hearts dictate our purposes, motivations, and priorities. Our actions reveal how firmly our heart is set.

We continually push God aside and find other things dominating our thoughts and inspirations. We want to control every aspect of our lives and set our hearts on things of our own desires. We worry about tomorrow despite God's promise to continually provide for us.

God's promise is great! When we set our hearts on His righteousness FIRST, all other things fall into place. The importance of our selfish desires pales in comparison to identifying with His kingdom. The relevance of our own control is diminished when we recognize the ultimate control and promises of God.

He must be the center of our focus FIRST. He must be our priority FIRST. He must be whom we trust FIRST. All things begin with God. He promises to take care of our needs when we set ourselves in Him. What we need to do is not confuse our wants with our needs.

When we set our hearts on ourselves instead of Him, we set ourselves up for disappointment and a shallowness of existence. His inspirations are pure and fill our lives with meaning, fullness, and purpose. Setting our hearts on Him FIRST gives perspective to our lives. Motivations change along with our contentment and devotion. True peace comes with dependence on Him. Joy and happiness stand close by. Set your heart on Him FIRST, and live a life of commitment, purpose, and peace. Depend on Him.

"God guides a man's steps
How could man discern the way he goes?"

PROVERBS 20:24

THE TESTIMONY

> *"This is the testimony: God has given us eternal life and this life is in His Son; anyone who has the Son has life, anyone who does not have the Son does not have life."*
>
> 1 JOHN 5:11-12

The testimony could not be more plain or direct. These two verses sum up very succinctly what life and faith are all about. There isn't a gray area.

Either you have the Son or you do not. You either put your future and faith in Him, or in yourself. So often we think that our futures can be directed by us rather than relying on what God has already given us. He has the perfect plan, and that plan is Christ. Plain and simple—eternal life is in Christ.

Do you have Christ? Will you participate in God's perfect plan, or will you sacrifice your eternal life with Him because you reject Christ? Would others say that your life reveals that you have Christ, or are your motivations based on a worldly view of success? Do you accept His gift, or do you want salvation on your own terms? These are tough questions that reveal so much about our commitments. What a great gift God has given us! Why do we try to make it so much more complicated than it is?

What does having the Son mean? It means acknowledging Christ as King and Savior of your life and soul. It means a commitment to Him in all areas of your life. It means to be humble in the realization that we are His children. It means a sacrificial heart, dedicated to being open to the opportunities to serve others that God puts before us each day and to dedicate our lives to being a witness to His truths to the world. It means living in contented peace in this world, knowing by faith that your eternal home is guaranteed by Christ's sacrifice, God's plan and love, and the Holy Spirit's guidance and strength.

What does not having the Son mean? It means continued disappointments in ourselves and those around us. It means a life focused on self, material advancement, and pride. It means anxiety, doubt, and guilt. It means being limited by our own understandings, emotions, and shortcomings. It means a life of loneliness and separation from hope.

Two distinctly different outcomes that are dependent on our acceptance of the gift of God, Christ. Which eternity will be yours? The testimony is clear and true. We have received a gift and we can make that gift ours by accepting Christ. He has offered Himself up for each of us. Take up His rich reward!

> *"He who despises the word will destroy himself,*
> *He who respects the commandment will be safe."*
>
> **PROVERBS 13:13**

THINK OUTSIDE OF YOURSELF

"Now after this He made His way through towns and villages preaching, and proclaiming the good News of the kingdom of God."

LUKE 8:1

Jesus did not wait for people to come to Him, He went to where the people were. He shared truth, inspired hope, and, most importantly, he gave of Himself. He was not on this earth for Himself, He was here for you and me. Too often we think we own our faith, making it so personal that we are not willing to go to where others are. You may believe, but can anyone tell? Do you make a difference? Every day we are traveling through our own "towns and villages" as we interact with those around us. Does your life preach and proclaim the Good News, or are you doing your best to blend in and be tolerant of the ideas of the world? There is no shortage of chances to walk in the steps of Jesus. Jesus did not demand that crowds follow Him. He planted seeds. He spoke the truth. He lived the life.

Not many verses after this verse, Jesus talks about how the seed will prosper depending on what kind of ground it falls on. He was spreading His seed everywhere, all the time, in every circumstance. It is up to us as followers of Christ to sow as many seeds as we can. No person is to be left out, and every type of soil needs to have contact with the seed. We can spread the seed if we will think outside of ourselves, and let our lives proclaim the Good News in whatever "town and village" we find ourselves. Our faith is not reserved for us alone; it is ours for the sharing. If we wait for others to come to us, we will miss chance after chance to be used by God. It will be by letting our faith get outside of ourselves that we can be the best instrument for Him. As Jesus was bold in His teaching, we too should be bold. Jesus was not afraid to be different. Jesus never backed down. Jesus spoke truth in every circumstance. Jesus was God, yet He did not sit back and wait to be worshipped. His mission and purpose was outside of Himself, for each of us. He came to us. He went to where the people were. Today He meets you where you are. Can you think outside of yourself, and meet others where they are? There are lots of seeds to sow.

> *"Do not say to your neighbor, 'Go away! Come another time! I will give it you tomorrow', if you can do it now."*
>
> **PROVERBS 3:28**

BE CURED

*"A leper came to Him and pleaded on his knees:
'If you want to,' he said, 'you can cure me.' Feeling sorry for him,
Jesus stretched out His hand and touched him.
'Of course I want to!' He said. 'Be cured!'"*

MARK 1:40

The leper was an outcast, suffering minute by minute as his body decayed. He was unclean and unloved. Society had shunned him and his infirmity was obvious to everyone. No one dared touch him. No one dared to be around him. He was the worst of the worst…except to Jesus.

This miracle performed by Jesus shows that none of us are outside His love. The leper came on his knees, submitting to the mercy of Jesus. He declared the authority of Jesus as the only source of power that was able to cure him. In a world that had given up on him, the leper put his trust and hope in both the person and the deity of Jesus. He came on his knees and pleaded for a miracle that would change his entire life. There was no one who could save him from his condition, except Jesus.

"Of course I want to!" He said. There have never been more soothing and loving words spoken to a man who needed Jesus more than ever. Jesus is near. Jesus is ready. Jesus cares. Jesus loves. When we find ourselves in times of desperation, He is close and available. When we have nowhere else to turn, He is waiting. When we bring ourselves to Him, He responds in love. The heart of Jesus is a heart of compassion and action. When we are at our worst, His words give us hope: "be cured!"

Jesus healed both the body and the spirit of the leper. He can do the same for us. Jesus heard the desperate pleas of a broken man. He does the same for us. Jesus showed mercy and compassion as He changed the life of the leper forever. He can do the same for us. Jesus has the power, authority, ability, and love to do miracles in our lives. He is ready to provide. Are you ready to ask?

> *"Do not think of yourself as wise, fear God and turn your back on evil: health-giving, this, to your body, relief to your bones."*
>
> PROVERBS 3:7-8

PSALM 136

Verses 1-3

"Alleluia!
Give thanks to God,
For He is good,
His love is everlasting!
Give thanks to the God of gods,
His love is everlasting!
Give thanks to the Lord of lords,
His love is everlasting!"

MY FOCUS

LANGUAGE OF THE CROSS

"The language of the cross may be illogical to those who are not on the way to salvation, but those of us who are on our way see it as God's power to save."

1 CORINTHIANS 1:18

How glorious is God's plan for our salvation! Would we be willing to endure the same sacrifices as Christ? No. Are we humans capable of providing and completing a plan for the salvation of the world? No. Does the mystery of God's plan go beyond our understanding? Yes. Can we as believers accept God's plan through faith? Yes!

Belief in ourselves and dependence on our own understanding leaves both the enormity and simplicity of God's plan too difficult for us to accept without faith. We want to be able to prove God's plan and hold His promises to an intellectual standard. Without faith, we cannot come to terms with the true meaning of Christ's sacrifice. On our own, we fail repeatedly and have nothing to give meaning to our lives. The depth of God's love is so far beyond our understanding and sinful nature that it just doesn't make sense.

The non-believer may demand proof, but what a believer has is so much better. We have hope. We have joy. We have faith. We know that our shortcomings and sins will not determine our eternity. It is an acceptance of

His salvation through faith that not only covers our sin, but outright cancels it. Christ's submission on the cross is the doorway to an eternal relationship with God. Too often we have a hard time allowing the power of the cross to change our lives. We think we have to do more and more to earn our salvation, when it has already been given to us.

When Christ said on the cross "It is finished," He completed all that is necessary. How could God love us so much? How could God's grace pay the price for our iniquity? It is this mystery that gives the cross so much power. It is this grace that cannot be explained by our own understanding, but instead relies on faith and acceptance. The power of the cross does not change your mind, it changes your heart. God's gift to us on the cross is not intellectual, it is relational. The acceptance of the cross makes us different creatures, not dependent on ourselves, but on Him. It is the only source of true peace. Listen to the language of the cross and let it change your heart. He has given the gift of salvation. Will you accept it?

> *"The hope of the wicked perishes with death,*
> *The expectation of the godless is frustrated."*

PROVERBS 11:7

STAND READY

"Therefore, you too must stand ready because the Son of Man is coming at an hour you do not expect."

MATTHEW 24:44

There is no time to waste. Now is the time to commit to a life in Christ. We do not know when, but we do know both the consequences if we fail to have a relationship with Christ and the joy of His fulfilled promises if we accept His grace.

Complacency creeps into our lives so easily even though we have God's Word to inspire us to action. Numerous worldly circumstances compete for and capture our attention away from the Almighty. It is so easy to become a lazy Christian. How do we keep our perspectives proper and our motives pure? This verse says it simply and clearly, "stand ready." We are to identify ourselves constantly and consistently as a child of God, ready and waiting for the return of Christ to earth. We are to be attentive and focused on being true Christians at all times. Our lives should be a display of the love of Christ through our actions, thoughts, and deeds. Being a Christian is not a part-time job. It is a willing commitment to a way of life. It is not a state of temporary acknowledgment; it is a dedication to His teachings and promises. It is not artificial or imposed; it is real and joyful. Each moment of life is precious and gives us the opportunity to identify ourselves with Christ.

Do you stand ready? If one minute from now the Lord returned, would you find yourself prepared? Would your heart and mind be ready to receive His grace? Could you stand before Him and give a proper account of yourself? There is no time to wait. There is no time to rationalize or procrastinate. The most important event in history could happen at any moment and we all must stand ready.

Readiness means being in harmony and communion with Christ. It means having faith in God's promises and the grace of Christ's sacrifice. It means dependence and trust, not in ourselves, but in Him. It means obedience, reliance, and a servant's heart. It means growing and maturing in the Word. It means glorifying God in all that we do. Do these characteristics describe your life at this moment in time? If not, it is time to get ready. The consequences are eternal. Stand ready!

"Do not boast about tomorrow,
Since you do not know what today will bring forth."

PROVERTBS 27:1

START WITH REPENTANCE

"From that moment Jesus began His preaching with the message, 'Repent, for the kingdom of heaven is close at hand.'"

MATTHEW 4:17

When we seek a relationship with God, where do we begin? Repentance. We are called directly by Jesus to recognize our sin, be remorseful for our sin, and to give ourselves over to a new Lord of our lives. We are called to change our behavior, attitude, and thinking as we approach His majesty. We need to build our foundation of relationship with Him on the bedrock of His power, justice, and grace. The time is now. The kingdom of heaven is close at hand.

Asking for forgiveness is an important component of humility. Humility is an active part of setting ourselves aside in order to depend upon the saving grace of God for our righteousness and salvation. Being sorry for our sins is necessary to give importance to our commitment to change and mold ourselves closer and closer to the image of Jesus. Sometimes it is not easy to say we are sorry. We hold on to our shortcomings as we try to minimize our failures. We become slaves to our own egos as we continue to be selfish in our actions. These attitudes keep us apart from God and push us into a routine of pride and comparison. Need to change direction? The first step is repentance.

Until we recognize and feel sorry for our selfishness, we cannot recognize the power and grace of God. Until we humble ourselves and attest to the majesty and love of God, we cannot experience the relationship with Him that He intends. Until we repent, we will miss the freedom that comes from being honest with God. It all starts with repentance.

The kingdom of God is always within our reach when we approach with an open heart, ready to receive the forgiveness God gives when we repent. We are promised the kingdom of God when we repent and receive the gift of grace that only God can provide. How do we start to rely and depend on God? Repent. How do we rid ourselves of the guilt of our sins? Repent. Where does our life of peace and joy find its source? It comes from our repentance and His grace. Jesus started His preaching with repentance as the focus for a reason. Repentance frees our hearts and sets us onto a path of relationship with the Almighty God. Find peace in His forgiveness and power in His strength. Repent and believe.

"The joy of the fool lies in doing wrong,
But the joy of the man of discernment is acquiring wisdom."

PROVERBS 10:23

THERE SHOULD BE LOVE

"The only purpose of this instruction is that there should be love, coming out of a pure heart, a clear conscience and a sincere faith."

1 TIMOTHY 1:5

The instruction that Paul is talking about in this verse is his request to Timothy to be sure that the Gospel message was being preached in its true form. Paul was concerned about false teachers, genealogies, and myths creeping into and taking away from the truth of the designs of God. Paul wanted to be sure that God's Word was unadulterated as people came to know Christ. Paul had a purpose: love.

Real love comes from a pure heart. There were to be no ulterior motives when it came to the Gospel. There were to be no hidden agendas and no self-serving platitudes. The reason to display this pure heart was to reflect the purity of God. He loves us despite ourselves. We love because we were first loved. We forgive because we were forgiven first. We believe because God never fails, is worthy, and is true. Our hearts are at the center of everything that we do. As a man's heart is, so shall he be. Let our hearts be pure and focused on love.

Guilt can be a life-determining emotion. It skews our way of thinking and our motivations. The Good News proclaimed that Christ has taken away the guilt of sin and created a new man within us. When we know and depend on God, we are new creatures, able to operate with the knowledge that past sins are forgiven and He understands our temptations, motivations, and shortcomings. Yes we as humans fail, but we can have a clear conscience as we know and rely on the promises of God to forgive us through Christ. We should not allow guilt to limit our ability to love. Feeling unloved does not preclude us from giving love. Belief in God's grace gives each of us the freedom to live as His children. Allow God to free your minds to love.

Our faith should be a palpable force in our lives. We live differently because of Christ. We live free because of Christ. We live loved because of Christ. The hope and joy of our salvation changes everything as our focus changes away from us and toward God. Our goals become eternal, not immediate. We live free to experience the joys of being children of God and not trying to be "good enough" to get to heaven. We know that even though we fail time after time, God does NOT fail. Because we depend on God and His love, we are totally free to also love.

For all of us, it can be a difficult thing to put ourselves aside and truly love. We all have our fears and anxieties that keep pushing our insecurities to the forefront. This verse encourages us to see past those issues and to rely on our faith in God for the ability to truly love. Only God can free our minds and spirits to be vehicles for His truth and love. He can free us from guilt and purify our hearts as we set out to do what God wants most. God is Love.

"My son, if your heart is wise,
Then my own heart is glad,
And my inmost self rejoices
When from your lips come honest words."

PROVERBS 23:15-16

BUT IF YOU SAY SO

"Master, Simon replied we worked hard all night long and caught nothing, but if you say so, I will pay out the nets."

LUKE 5:5

Is your net ever empty? Have you worked hard, applying your knowledge and expertise only to come up short of your expectations? Despite those feelings of inadequacies, have you ever simply just done what Jesus asks of you? A catch that could fill your nets is on the other side of that kind of obedience.

Before Jesus called him into discipleship, Simon was a lifelong fisherman, knowing when and how to make his catch, yet this night came back empty. How frustrating after a hard night's work to return empty-handed. Yet it was this failure that was used as the vehicle to teach many the power of Jesus and the rewards of obedience. It was Simon's boat that Jesus used as his podium to teach. It was at a disappointing time for Simon that Jesus would use that circumstance to change history. It was at Simon's discouraging moment that Jesus used that time to reveal Himself and the rewards for obedience.

Of course Simon resisted at first, just like all of us would. In essence Simon says, "You've got to be kidding me! I worked all night and came up with nothing. I am the fisherman here; you Jesus are just a carpenter's son. I can control my own life." But he doesn't stop there as most of us would. With the words, "but if you say so," Simon's life changes forever. How many times have all of us stopped short of uttering those words? We may not like our present conditions, our relationships, the direction our life is going, or a myriad of other complaints. But why not go a few words further? "But if you say so." Those words are a powerful commitment of obedience. No further explanations needed. No debate. No rationalization. No other reasons needed. "But if you say so" is all we need. Just like Simon, we all find ourselves at points of disappointment and frustration. Despite our best efforts, things do not always go as planned, and we must come to terms with the fact that we cannot control every aspect of our lives. Our challenge is that when we do find ourselves at these points in our lives, we need to know where to turn for answers that will not only satisfy, but will overflow. Simon acted. He did what Jesus told him to do, and he was rewarded with a catch so big he couldn't even haul it in his boat. His faith and obedience resulted in not just a change in the number of fish caught, it resulted in him falling on his knees in front of the One who changed his life forever. That day Simon was overcome by the power of God to change him. What will it take for each of us to be overcome, to realize that God is above all circumstances and in every situation?

Too often we want to make things so difficult. We find convoluted explanations and reasons to rationalize our actions. We try to fit God into our plans for what we have determined to be best for us. We rely on ourselves, planning our futures and trying to match our motives with our ideas. Simon's example tells us there is a better way. Simon didn't overanalyze anything. He obeyed. He didn't question Jesus. He acted. As we go about our life, let us commit our actions to God's way, and acknowledge that these five words spoken by Simon can change our whole relationship with God. Doubt is natural, but our response must put faith in the Most High. He may ask you to do things outside your comprehension. "But if you say so."

> *"Commend what you do to God,*
> *And your plans will find achievement."*

PROVERBS 16:3

PERFECTION

"I am no longer trying for perfection by my own efforts, the perfection that comes from the Law, but I want only the perfection that comes through faith in Christ, and is from God and based on faith."

PHILIPPIANS 3:9

How useless and condemning are your own efforts to find perfection by your own actions! How glorious and liberating is the perfection we have based on faith!

These two different ideas of how to obtain perfection will define you. You can either be the center of your being and trust yourself to find a way to perfection, or you can humble yourself before God and allow your faith in the sacrifices of Christ to be your way to perfection. There is no gray area. You either trust yourself or you trust God.

The decision you make about who to trust will define how you act, how you think, and what you say. It will determine your focus, emotions, and the peace you find. We can strive for perfection in everything that we do, but we will always come up short. Even though our efforts may be honorable and our ideals noble, trusting in our own abilities is a pathway to failure. But the promises of God and the sacrifices of Christ can bring us to a perfection that we can never know on our own. Our own ideas of perfection have little to do with the perfection that comes through faith in Christ. What we consider important so often is not based on faith and our reliance on the promises of God.

Relax!! Through your faith, God has provided you with a means of peace and perfection. Let Him bring you to perfection.

"God guides a man's steps:
How could man discern the way he goes?"

PROVERBS 20:24

PSALM 19

Verses 7-8

Verse 14

"The Law of God is perfect,
New life for the soul;
The decree of God is trustworthy,
Wisdom for the simple.
The precepts of God are upright,
Joy for the heart;
The commandment of God is clear,
Light for the eyes."

"May the words of my mouth always find favour,
And the whispering of my heart, in Your presence, God,
My rock, my redeemer."

MY FOCUS

THE TIME TO REPENT IS NOW

"Your stubborn refusal to repent is only adding to the anger God will have towards you on that day of anger when His just judgements will be made known. He will repay each one as his works deserve."

ROMANS 2:5-6

Pride is a major obstacle to our relationship with God. In our stubborn attitude, we continue to try to put ourselves first, diminishing the rightful place of the Almighty. In these verses, Paul is talking to an audience that knows how to come into relationship with God, but refuses to do so. They were relying on their own methods toward salvation, rather than leaning into God's plan for them. They wanted to play by their own rules, relying on themselves, rather than holding fast to the grace of God. We do the same thing day after day, striving to complete our personal agendas, rather than responding to God in whatever situation we find ourselves. Where is our humility? Where is our commitment to serve? What honor to God does our life reveal?

Repentance is an essential element to our salvation. Sinful in nature, there is nothing that we could ever do that would cover all our sins to allow us to be heirs with Christ in eternity. The act of repentance shows that we recognize our frailties and realize there is only one way toward justification and redemption…Christ. Repentance is a word of action, having at its core the motivation to change the way we live. It is recognizing that we fall short of perfection, need to put our faith and hope in Christ, and need to commit ourselves to do all we can to actively align with Christ and His example.

Our good works cannot earn our way to heaven, but unrepentant bad works will have a consequence. Good works are an indication of where our hearts are, not a checklist toward salvation. Once we have repented, sin loses its power. Christ has already paid the full price for it. It is remembered no more. What comfort we can find in the truth and power of Christ!

What are we waiting for? How long does it take to truly, fully commit to the grace that God has provided for all? How long will we put our own agendas, failures, and self-reliance ahead of a life of victory in Christ? These verses warn us emphatically that God cannot be fooled and will not take second place to our egos. God is supreme, just, and fair. Each of us has the ability and path to choose God over ourselves. Each of us can commit ourselves to a life of service rather than expecting to be served. Each of us has the ability to repent. The time is now to stop refusing and let God be God.

"Do not think of yourself as wise,
Fear God and turn your back on evil."

PROVERBS 3:7

NOT BREAD ALONE

"Man does not live on bread alone, but on every word that comes from the mouth of God."

MATTHEW 4:4

True life is not just existence. True life is full of experience and has depth and meaning because we have a soul. Created in God's image, we were formed and designed to be beings with the capacity for relationship and the ability to recognize that our existence has a purpose and meaning. We are much more than a biological reality...we are a child of the Almighty God.

It is very obvious that we need to have, at minimum, a food source to survive. But we are meant to do more than merely survive. Bread does not feed our conscience, ambitions, or spirit. Bread does not feed our compassion, empathy, or our ability to love. Bread does not feed our relationships, feelings, or our ability to believe in something we cannot see. Bread is necessary, but meaningless without God.

There is a big difference between being alive and living. Living life to its fullest requires God. His promises, comfort, and truth provide the foundation for us to experience life in the manner that He intended. We were designed for relationship, full of emotion. We were created to worship, able to acknowledge the existence of God. We were made to love, using Christ as our example.

Are we living our lives to the fullest or just existing? Have we allowed ourselves to experience all that God has provided to us? Where do we get our food? This verse makes it very clear that the nourishment we really need comes directly from the mouth of God. Every word of God is food for us that nourishes our inner being. With God as our source of energy, we can live with meaning and purpose.

Let God be the source of power in your life and enjoy the fullness He has intended for each of us. It is time to stop just being alive. It is time to live, truly live, in the fullness and depth of life that God has for each of us.

> *"The blessings of God is what brings riches,*
> *To this hard toil has nothing to add."*
>
> PROVERBS 10:22

DO NOT DISOWN HIM

"But the one who disowns Me in the presence of men,
I will disown in the presence of My Father in heaven."

MATTHEW 10:33

I am a follower of Christ! How often do these words come up in your daily conversations? In today's world, declarations of faith are seldom talked about and, in some crowds, can be considered inappropriate. Society wants to separate our faith from our decisions and actions. For a Christian, this is impossible! Consider if your words and life boldly declare that "I am a Christian."

Declare it in your home. Let your daily devotions and time spent in the Word set the foundation of a Christian home. Dedicate your home to be a place where God dwells. Lead by example as your children see a person committed to making moral and God-based decisions on a daily basis.

Declare yourself a Christian at your place of work. Let humility, honesty, integrity, and a godly attitude shine brightly in the face of the pressures to compromise. Fight the temptations that a secular world continues to put in front of you. Do what is right!

Declare yourself a Christian with your friends. Your words, actions, and willingness to help those in need can shout loudly that Christ is in your heart.

Comforting friends and being available to them in times of need is a much needed and appreciated ministry.

Declare yourself a Christian in your community. Happy sacrifice and humble commitment to those who live around us, even if we don't know them personally, spreads the holy promises of God and fulfills our charge to bring others to Christ. Let God use you to bring the good news of Christ to those whom you can touch. A committed Christian happily declares Christ in the presence of men. He is in you. Declare it!

There are so many pressures today to not declare ourselves for Christ. Politicians want God out of the decision-making process. Society demands tolerance to such a degree that you are not allowed to declare yourself for Christ for fear of infringing on someone else's rights. Declaring Christ *is* the right thing to do! Daily efforts are underway to take Christ out of our lives. This verse could not be any plainer and the warning is not ambiguous. Do not expect Christ to declare you if you will not declare Him. Being a Christian is not a vocation that you leave and pick up again. It is not only appropriate in certain circumstances. Being a Christian is who we are and demands declaration through everything that we do. Do not be ashamed or embarrassed, but declare it proudly by your words, deeds, and priorities. I am a Christian!

> *"Commend what you do to God,*
> *And your plans will find achievement."*

PROVERBS 16:3

THE TRUE GOD

"We know, too, that the Son of God has come, and has given us the power to know the true God. We are in the true God, as we are in His Son, Jesus Christ. This is the true God, this is eternal life."

1 JOHN 5:20

We *know*. It is a fact. It is the Truth. He has come. We can know Him. He is eternal life. When we call ourselves a Christian we are not identifying with a movement, a theology, or an idea. We are identifying with Him, the person of Christ. Too often we spend our time learning about Him, forgetting that the real goal is to know not just about Him, but really know Him. John saw the true God in person and wanted to remind everyone that when they see Jesus, they see the fullness of God. John declares that he knows as absolute truth that Jesus was the true God. In Jesus we see the fullness of God and the mercy He shows us by letting us know Him at an intimate level. God allowed us, His creation, to see Him in the flesh and see His mercy and grace personally. We have been allowed to see the love of God in action in the person of Jesus. How blessed we are.

All power rests with God. Not only can Jesus give us eternal life, He is eternal life! He is the fullness of grace. He is the fullness of love. We are allowed to experience God in the person of Jesus. His blood is our path, and

His power to forgive is our salvation. He allows us to know Him, personally and passionately. We can have complete confidence in our eternity because of Him.

In a world that struggles to know what truth really is, it is refreshing to see the confidence of John when he declares that the reality of Christ is absolutely the truth. It is hard in this world to depend on anything, but we can find sure footing when we accept the truth of Jesus. Absolute truth is Jesus.

Our true God is a personal God. He speaks to each of us with the same love, the same compassion, and the same grace. He comes directly to us, waiting for us to use the power He has given us to believe. What a gift it is to have a God that wants us to know Him personally. In Him is power, truth, and eternal life. In Him there is salvation, righteousness, and grace. In Him we are saved.

> *"Fear of God gives good grounds for confidence,*
> *In Him, His children find a refuge."*
>
> PROVERBS 14:26

ONE PERFECT OFFERING

"By virtue of that one single offering, He has achieved the eternal perfection of all who He is sanctifying."

HEBREWS 10:14

Christ did it all, once and for all. His suffering, death, and resurrection wipes away the need for our continuing sacrifices to atone for our sins. He did it all, and it was perfect. Christ laid the foundation for our ability to be considered holy and our claim to live free under His blood. His offering was superior in every way, complete in every way, and perfect in every way. This is the foundation for our step-by-step process toward holiness that God has always intended. This is the freedom to live as saved souls rather than condemned sinners. His restorative grace is the one perfect offering that puts us back into relationship with Him. One perfect offering.

Without the perfect offering of Christ, we would all be in a perpetual state of regret and guilt, trying desperately to figure out how to pay for our sin. Nothing we could do would ever be good enough. But Christ changed that, forever, with the one perfect offering of Himself. His perfection covers our imperfection, and His grace covers our failures. His mercy gives us freedom and His love overpowers our weakness. Only because of His one perfect offering are we able to approach God with confidence and assuredness. He made it all possible. One perfect offering.

What this offering did for us was let us live free and able to look at life not through the lens of potential failure, but instead a lens of becoming closer and closer to God. We are forgiven, but too often forget to live like it. Sanctification is a process of becoming more and more holy, molding ourselves with the help of the Holy Spirit into someone who reflects the character of Christ. Christ made it possible for us to focus on grace rather than sin, relationship rather than works, and obedience rather than sacrifice. Forgiven believers live with an eye on thanksgiving, service, obedience, and hope. They can live freely to love abundantly and be sure of their salvation. Christ has done the work. His one single offering is sufficient. His mercy and grace have covered our sins of the past, present, and future. One perfect offering.

As children of God, we share in the work of our Lord Jesus Christ. We are co-heirs with Christ and reap the benefits of His one perfect offering. Our focus can therefore be on taking on more of the character of Christ each and every day as we strive for closer and closer relationship with Him. We will never reach perfection on this side of heaven, but because of the one perfect offering of Christ, we are free to mature and grow in our faith without the guilt of our sin. He took care of that. We can strive to live to embrace Christ instead of fearing sin. We can move forward with trust without the regrets of sin holding us back. His one perfect offering is His gift to all of us through faith. Hold that gift tightly and grow in faith as a forgiven child of God. Because of His one perfect offering.

> *"To act virtuously and with justice*
> *is more pleasing to God than sacrifice."*

PROVERBS 21:3

REDEEM THIS AGE

"This may be a wicked age, but your life should redeem it."

EPHESIANS 5:16

Beyond any doubt, this is an age of wickedness. God continues to be pushed further and further from importance as man struggles to be in charge of every situation. The age scoffs at sacrificial behavior, characterizing it as a weakness. Ego and self-importance become drivers for our short-sighted goals. We seek comfort and advantage instead of obedience and humbleness.

What are we to do? This verse tells us not to give in to the wicked, warped worldview. It is by the way you live your life that you give meaning to the promises of God. It is within our ability, through the Holy Spirit, to make a difference in this world. The circumstances that we find ourselves in should not dictate our behavior. If we are committed to doing what is right in the eyes of God, we will impact our society.

Numerous times throughout each and every day we have decisions to make and a choice of gods to serve. Do we treat our resources as our own earned property, or are they only on loan to us by God in order to provide us the opportunity to be good stewards of His gifts? Is it alright to cheat or let an error go unmentioned if it is to our benefit, or does honesty and doing the right thing bring an unsurpassed peace to our heart? Does the political system and magnitude of our national problems leave you feeling powerless, or do your relationships have a depth that can only come when you are filled with Christ living in you? There is only one God to serve, the Almighty God.

This may be a wicked age, but that does not mean that we give in to wickedness. God has set the standard high, but He has also given us all the tools we need for success. Our goal should be to always improve every situation, putting the best construction on every circumstance. God gives us opportunities to be His followers in even the worst of times. The wickedness of this world may touch our circumstances, but it cannot alter our hearts and souls. Stop worrying about the wickedness around you, and focus on LIVING the life that God has in mind for you.

Your acts of kindness and love can defeat a world of wickedness. Carry the power of Christ's redeeming love with you and you will always be whole.

"Their virtuous conduct sets honest men free,
Treacherous men are imprisoned by their own desires."

PROVERBS 11:6

PSALM 42

Verses 1-4

"As a doe longs for running streams,
So longs my soul for You, my God.
My soul thirsts for God,
The God of life;
When shall I go to see the face of God?
I have no food but tears, day and night;
And all day long men say to me,
'Where is your God?'
I remember, and my soul melts with me;
I am on my way to the wonderful Tent,
To the house of God,
Among cries of joy and praise
And an exultant throng."

MY FOCUS

THE SAME

"Jesus Christ is the same today as He was yesterday and as He will be forever."

HEBREWS 13:8

When we put our trust and faith in Christ, it can be forever. The nature of Christ never changes. While ideas, customs, and traditions may change over time, Christ does not change. We have all seen the latest fads come and go. We have seen new theologies make a splash, then fade away. We have seen the newest idea become an afterthought overnight. We put our hopes in a new technology, a new leader, or a new philosophy only to be disappointed time and time again. Christ has not and will not disappoint.

So often we look for outward means of salvation or a way to make our lives easier. We get frustrated when we realize we cannot control every facet of our lives. The only thing that never changes is Christ. Christ is the only trustworthy answer. His promises are true and constant. His grace is present and continues. His atonement is for us, forever. His sacrifice is sufficient for all eternity. In what and in whom do you trust? Stop being disappointed by the world and find the joy that comes with making Christ your king.

Worldly influences and influencers come and go. There is a pundit around every corner telling us what we should know, how we should perceive, and trying to conform us to their way of thinking. They will be wrong most of the time. In contrast, Christ has always told the truth, lived the perfect life, and reigns in heaven with the Father in perfection. His truth does not change. Absolute truth is impossible to find apart from God. God's truth is not situational or malleable. It is purely true.

Take a step back today, and ask yourself what you trust. Is it something you think you can control, or is it in the omnipotent Christ? Do you trust in something that will give you temporary gain, or in the Savior that gives you the eternal gift of salvation? Choose Christ.

> *"Fear of God gives good grounds for confidence,*
> *In Him, His children find a refuge."*
>
> **PROVERBS 14:26**

FREE TO CHOOSE

"For me there are not forbidden things; maybe, but not everything does good. I agree there are no forbidden things for me, but I am not going to let anything dominate me."

1 CORINTHIANS 6:12

Our salvation is not dependent upon a set of rules and regulations that we must follow in order to meet the requirements necessary. Because we are forgiven children of God, we are given the freedom to live apart from legal edicts and judgments. But with the great power of freedom comes the equally great responsibility to use it wisely. Make certain you are using your freedom for the benefit of God's kingdom. As it is often said, just because you can doesn't mean you do.

Real freedom releases us from living by regulation and replaces it with living for the opportunity to serve. We are not bound to follow a set of laws; we are free to experience a commonality with Christ. When we are free, we are judged by our hearts, which allows us to use our freedoms with wisdom and purpose. Not exercising freedom is sometimes the most powerful action we can take. Restraint and obedience are signs of the understanding of what freedom in Christ really is. In our freedom, we gladly accept being a slave to Christ. In a world full of choices, we are the most free when we choose Christ.

There are so many things in this world that take our focus off of Christ. They steal our attention and shape our responses in ways that can pull us away from faith. Do not let those things put you under their influence and dominate your thoughts. Be a wise and thoughtful person, putting Christ above all else.

When our only motive is to follow Christ, we are free. When we make purposeful decisions to see things through the lens of Christ, we are truly free. When we decide to let Christ rule our life, we are truly free.

"Their virtuous conduct sets honest men free,
Treacherous men are imprisoned by their own desires."

PROVERBS 11:6

NO MORE LIES

"So from now on there must be no more lies: You must speak the truth to one another, since we are all parts of one another."

EPHESIANS 4:25

Truth, the whole truth, and nothing but the truth. Is this lip service to an ideal, a slogan that has lost its meaning?

Truth cannot be rationalized and it is not subject to various definitions. Truth is truth, based on a knowledge of genuine right and wrong, fairness, and honesty. Truth is not based on motives and cannot be turned and twisted to make it more palatable.

So many times we want the truth to be something it isn't. The truth of our shortcomings faces us every day. The truth of our selfishness is evident by the way we prioritize our lives. The truth of our sin puts us on our knees to ask for forgiveness.

This verse couldn't be more clear—there must be no more lies! How else can we build trust with each other if we cannot rely on telling the truth to each other? Trust is a fragile, important commodity. It is built up by repeated truths that give us a level of confidence of honesty. The unfortunate thing is trust can be damaged so easily when a lie breaks the pattern of truth, and it takes time and effort to rebuild the failed trust that lies have destroyed.

Too often we get caught up in self-advancement and try to bend the truth to suit the circumstances best for ourselves. We are so easily embarrassed by our shortcomings that we use our own version of the truth to blame someone else for our failures. We look to place blame on others, when instead we should be taking responsibility for our own actions.

There is no circumstance for a Christian to lie. Obviously there are times when situations need to be handled with understanding and compassion, but our word MUST be trustworthy.

All of us in this world are interrelated. We are all God's creations, are valuable in God's eyes, and have a purpose. Each and every lie works against God and His children.

Speak truth with authority and compassion. Let it be known by example that your words are trustworthy. God is our example. He speaks the truth and we know we can depend on Him and His promises. Be honest before God and men. Your pure heart and trustworthiness can then be used by God to advance His truths. Represent Him with the truth!

"The false witness will always find his doom,
But the speech of the obedient will always be heard."

PROVERBS 21:28

LIVE AT PEACE

Do all that you can to live at peace with everyone."

ROMANS 12:18

Living at peace with fellow believers is easy.
Living at peace with those that agree with me is easy.
Living at peace with those that disagree with me is not so easy.
Living at peace with those that hate me is hard.

This simple verse is short, but demanding. We are called to do everything we possibly can to live in peace with everyone, no matter what. God is the God of all, the Savior of all, and the source of mercy and grace for all. We only need to focus on our response to the love of God as we seek harmony and peace with all creation. We live in a time when disagreements are magnified and sensationalized to the point of dividing people. It seems as though our society thrives on conflict and disagreement, rewarding the loudest voice in the room and the most controversial. We, however, are called to peace.

We spend a lot of time comparing ourselves with other people, trying to put ourselves ahead and above whoever does not meet our expectations. We spend too much time looking for differences rather than similarities, shortcomings rather than talents, and negativity rather than blessings. It is up to us to do all that we can to mirror the love of Christ to everyone. Every part of God's creation deserves to be treated with dignity and compassion. God does not distinguish between rich or poor, strong or weak. His life, death, and resurrection allow all of those with faith in Him to put aside differences with others and be at peace. A peacemaker has the heart of God. A peacemaker shows he has faith, trust, and respect for God. Being a peacemaker is our obligation as a believer and an honor as a child of God. Be at peace with everyone, including God.

Bitterness is in the heart of the schemer,
Joy with those who give counsels of peace."

PROVERBS 12:20

THE RIGHT COURSE

*Be careful always to choose the right course;
be brave under trials; make the preaching of the Good News
your life's work, in thoroughgoing service."*

2 TIMOTHY 4:5

Every day (and often many times a day) we have choices. We continually have to decide which course we will take. How do you choose? What criteria do you use to make your decisions? How does your relationship to God influence your thinking and actions? This verse gives you the basis on which you can decide your course. In every situation your actions and words are preaching your values to those around you. Does your life preach the Good News? Does your life testify to your complete commitment to service for God?

One thing you can be sure of, you will be tested. The right course may not be the easiest or most popular. The right course may demand sacrifice and humbleness. The right course may take courage. Be brave! Stand firm! Always, always take the right course!

The course you will choose will depend on where you are heading. A path leading to a worldly goal is a much different path than the one that leads to preaching the Good News. Is the course you are on leading you to the

Good News? Do your daily decisions promote you, or God? This verse tells us our service to God should be thoroughgoing. The right course is chosen because your commitment to God is complete and your motivations are pure. The right course is chosen because you stand firm under trials and gladly identify with the promises of the Good News. The right course is chosen because your life is focused on godly things and you understand that God is your first priority.

Will it be easy? No. But it will be obedient, courageous, and right. Your life can make a statement for God. Carefully consider the course of your life. Wherever you are and whatever your circumstances, the course you choose will influence others. It will preach a message, so be sure it is the message of the Good News. Humble yourself to thoroughgoing service to God and you will take the right course.

*"A man's heart plans his own way,
But it is God who makes his steps secure."*

PROVERBS 10:9

STAND

"Happy the man who stands firm when trials come."

JAMES 1:12

Persevering through hardship is satisfying, building, and honorable. Not letting yourself be swayed by current opinion when you know the truth is a sign of strength and dedication. Letting your faith be your source of strength in the face of adversity shows reliance and commitment to God. Making it through hardships, without losing sight of the Truth, yields a happy heart.

Everywhere we turn we are being challenged as believers. Society is doing its best to make God not only irrelevant, but foolish as well. In a world struggling for power, it forgets that the source of all power is God, and that humility and service are virtues to be sought after. We must persist in our commitment to faith above all else. We as believers own the solid ground in Jesus Christ. We as believers will overcome because our solution is eternal. We as believers find a peace and joy that the world cannot understand. No matter what challenges we face, we can continue to act in love because the source of our happiness, Jesus Christ, has all the power.

It is so easy to be swayed and manipulated by all that goes on around us. We are pressured by the media, motives, and a false narrative that *we* are the answer to the problems of the world. We need to look to Christ. We look for people to solve our issues and make our lives better. We need to look to Christ. Politicians and intellectuals are not the answer. We need to look to Christ.

Those that stand firm find happiness and contentment in the power of Christ. That power provides peace and an understanding that happiness is not determined by circumstance, it is found in faith. Resting in the truth of Christ and the forgiveness we receive from Him lets us live happy and free, knowing we have already conquered the effect of any trial. Trials come, but they cannot steal the happiness of faith. Trials grab our attention and zap our strength, but they cannot overcome the power of Christ to save and protect our hearts.

The anxiety that trials bring cannot compare to the happiness that is found in the character of Christ and the fulfillment found in reliance on Him. When we feel ourselves slipping away, we can find real happiness knowing that the solid ground of Christ is always within grasp and will always hold fast. Standing firm builds confidence and perseverance builds character. No matter what the circumstance or challenge, our foundation and future are secure. So stand tall and strong in the Lord, never backing away from the truth of His salvation. Love freely in spite of what challenges are present and smile. God is on your side.

> *"When the storm is over, the wicked man is no more,*
> *But the virtuous stands firm forever."*
>
> **PROVERBS 10:25**

PSALM 96

Verses 1-6

"Sing God a new song!
Sing to God, all the earth!
Sing to God, bless His name.
Proclaim His salvation day after day,
Tell of His glory among the nations,
Tell His marvels to every people.
God is great, loud must be His praise,
He is to be feared beyond all gods.
Nothingness, all the gods of the nations.
God Himself made the heavens,
In His presence are splendor and majesty,
In His sanctuary power and beauty."

MY FOCUS

THE REAL WREATH

"All the fighters at the games go into strict training; they do this to win a wreath that will wither away, but we do it for a wreath that will never wither."

1 CORINTHIANS 9:25

What does it take to be a winner? Winning is a combination of very difficult tasks: hard work, commitment, the willingness to take instruction, honest self-assessment, training, and focus. Do these words describe the effort we put into our faith?

As I was throwing away my old high school athletic trophies I was reminded of all the practices and time I spent being part of a team that was focused on winning. I remembered how proudly I received the trophies and felt the excitement and satisfaction of a job well done. I was a winner and the proof was up on the shelf. The trophy had meaning to me, but had no impact on anyone else. Those emblems are now just mementos headed for the trash. I had won, but the victory had withered away.

So why is it that we think that the most important prize of all, our relationship with Christ, will just come to us without us putting in the work? We need to be prepared for Him, willing to commit to the strict training of obedience required. Unlike the trophies we worked so hard for that faded away, all our effort will be meaningful and rewarded as we hone our hearts to be receptive to the grace of God. We have in Christ the prize that never withers, always loves, and impacts others. We have in Christ the prize that loves unconditionally and eternally, strengthens universally and personally, and completes us with grace and mercy. Christ is the prize that never withers and never loses its value. Christ is the ultimate victory. He is worthy of our training.

Are you willing to work hard for Christ, proactively proclaiming His victory? Will you commit your time and energy to the Almighty? Are you willing to be corrected in love for your benefit? Will you dedicate your life to Him? Can you see the things around you that tempt and drag you away from faith, then move yourself back to Him? Can your daily routine include Christ? Can you never lose sight of Him, seeing all things through the lens of Christ?

So many things in life that we think are important end up to be trophies in the trash. Our misguided goals can pull us away from Christ, dwindling away our strength, stamina, and energy. Instead, let us all be willing to be trained for Christ, letting His strength do the heavy lifting. Let His love give the peace and comfort that the world cannot provide. Let His grace overwhelm you to a life of freedom and peace of mind. Let Him be the prize. May we all be victorious.

> *"The horse is made ready for the day of battle,*
> *But victory rests with the Lord."*

PROVERBS 21:31

SECRET PLACE

"But when you pray, go to your private room and, when you have shut your door, pray to your Father who is in that secret place, and your Father who sees all that is done in secret will reward you."

MATTHEW 6:6

God, our Father, wants a personal relationship with each one of us. He doesn't want prayer for show or prayers of recitation. He wants personal communication; prayers that come from our hearts and not from memorization. He wants us to be the means for bringing His heavenly will to earth.

This secret place where God meets you is your place of truth. It is the place where you acknowledge that God knows your heart and motivations. It is there that the truth about your trust comes to light. Do you put yourself ahead of God? It is the place where your sins and desires are laid bare. Are you still trying to hide sins and failures from God? You cannot lie or hide from the truth that God knows. You may be able to fool people around you, but God knows your heart, where secrets cannot be hidden. Too many of us lead double lives, fooling those around us into a false image of who we truly are. God cannot be fooled. Sometimes we are even so good at hiding or making excuses for our sin that we fool ourselves. God cannot be fooled.

Be honest with God. Be genuine. Be transparent. God wants to meet our needs, but first we must ask. We must ask in honesty, humbleness, and trust. We must acknowledge the deity of God and His position as our ultimate provider. Through our honest prayer and honest relationship with God we become representatives of His will here on earth through the Holy Spirit.

It is time for openness and honesty with God. He knows our needs. He is waiting for us to ask, to acknowledge our dependence on Him. His promise is great. He promises to hear us. He knows us and sees us when we desire Him. Prayer should not be done out of obligation, routine, or convenience. Prayer is our means for an intimate, personal relationship with God. He sees you. He knows you. He will reward you. Get to know Him.

"He whose course is honest fears God,
He whose paths are crooked scorns Him."

PROVERBS 14:2

THE TIME OF COMFORT

"Now you must repent and turn to God, so that your sins may be wiped out, and so that the Lord may send the time of comfort."

ACTS 3:19

A season of comfort is a universal need in our world today. We are surrounded by conflict and hate, jealousy and the quest for power. We desperately need to take a deep breath and reassess our priorities and loyalties. The priorities and conditions of this world do not offer a chance of rest. We need to be covered with the assurances of God and find rest in Him. We need God more than ever. Repenting is sometimes not an easy thing to do. Pride and self-sufficiency lead us to think that we are always in the right and we can do everything by ourselves. We hate to admit we are wrong. We hate to be told that our way is not the best way. We want to buy into the worldly concept that truth is somehow malleable. We often do not allow the absolute truth of Jesus to be our daily guide. We need a different path.

Turn to God. This is a simple solution that has so many implications to our lives. Everything changes when we turn to God. Putting others before ourselves? That is a God thing. Acknowledging that we have sinned and committing to strive to live a more godly life. That is a God thing. Being humble, listening before speaking, showing compassion. These are God things.

And loving is the biggest God thing of all. It seems that we are consumed by putting self above everything else, trying to find our worth in ourselves. Our worth comes from being a son or daughter of God, happily showing the love of God in all that we do to all people. Turning to God will change everything.

What happens when we turn to God? The guilt, the oppression of our sins, and the weight of our inadequacy are all wiped out. And many things are received! We get joy, peace, rest, peace, hope, trust, and assuredness. We get eternal life, patience, and freedom. Turning to God changes everything.

Christ is the great Comforter. He can restore your peace and joy. He can give you rest. We have a comforter in Jesus Christ.

> *"He who conceals his faults will not prosper,*
> *He who confesses and renounces them will find mercy."*
>
> PROVERBS 28:13

SINCERE LOVE

"Love must be sincere. Hate what is evil; cling to what is good."

ROMANS 12:9

Superficial love is easy. Sincere love requires active compassion. Sincere love means taking up a mantle of humility. We must concern ourselves with others and give value and urgency to their needs. Compassion and empathy for others without the thought of repayment requires pure intentions. Can you actively find and meet the needs of someone else today without regard to the personal cost to yourself?

Do you really hate evil or do you rationalize tolerance? We are instructed not to tolerate, condone, or ignore any form of evil. We are instructed to hate evil. We can do so much to harm the kingdom of God by our apathy toward evil. Do not just step aside from evil or look the other way. You must flee from it. Then, find what is good and anchor yourself to it. Be identified with what is pure and good and distance yourself from evil.

Today we will have many opportunities to identify ourselves with what is good and right. Let us cling to these chances with sincere love. Let our closeness to God be our identity so that the kingdom of God can be furthered. Pray for the wisdom to recognize evil and the strength to recognize and cling to good. Pray that your love would be sincere.

We all have a choice to make every day. Do you embrace what is good? Do you recognize and flee from evil? Do you treat others with sincere love? We know that our strength comes from God whose love is sincere and He is good. Cling to Him.

*"No man is secure by wickedness,
but nothing shakes the roots of virtuous men."*

PROVERBS 12:3

REMAIN

> *"So then, my brothers and dear friends, do not give way but remain faithful in the Lord. I miss you very much, dear friends; you are my joy and my crown."*
>
> PHILIPPIANS 4:1

There are times when simply remaining faithful can be the most difficult thing to do. We may know we have faith in God, but we get pulled in many directions. We may know we trust God, but the wear and tear of everyday life makes us lose our focus. We know that we are always loved by God, but there are times when He seems far away. There are times in all of our lives that we let our emotions get in the way of our trust in God. What do we do when our faith seems to erode away? We must remain.

We cannot always be in a deep, emotional relationship with God. Our faith life has its ups and downs, but we cannot forget that God is always there. We're going to sin, to doubt, and to trust in ourselves alone. How do we cope when happiness has slipped away? We must remain.

There are so many things that try to steal our joy. Daily we face a constant barrage of trials and temptations. We see anger and discontent around us as anxiousness and turmoil increase. We may face illness or pain, loss or disappointment, yet He is always there. How can we keep an attitude of thanksgiving through all these challenges? We must remain.

We live in a time when God is being pushed away from society with many leaders finding no place for Him. We try to find human solutions to problems that can only be answered through faith in Him. We see inequity and injustice, the lack of common sense and reason, selfishness, and a thirst for power rule the day. How can we find worth in a time when so many devalue the power of God? We must remain.

Happiness may temporarily evade us, but the joy of a loving Father in heaven is always present. We do have value, because we are loved by God. We do have purpose, because He has placed you exactly where you are right now for His reasons. We do have power within us as the Holy Spirit moves us to action. We may live in the day, but we serve for an eternal purpose. How can we overcome this world? We must remain.

There is only one thing worthy of our total commitment and dedication: God Almighty. There is only one thing that rules supreme with justice and love: God Almighty. There is only one thing constant in the universe: God Almighty. In Him we can find peace in times of trouble and joy in times of hardship. In Him alone we must remain.

> *"Do not let your hearts be envious of sinners*
> *But be steady every day in the fear of God."*
>
> **PROVERBS 23:17**

GLORY IS YOUR DESTINY

"I think that what we suffer in this life can never be compared to the glory, as yet unrevealed, which is waiting for us. The whole creation is eagerly waiting for God to reveal His sons."

ROMANS 8:18

Glory is your destiny! A glory that is so much greater than any suffering here on earth awaits you. Doesn't this verse give you a great promise of hope? We all have our own sufferings and can spend so much of ourselves involved in dealing with them. How much greater than these sufferings is the glory that awaits you which is promised by God?

Sin is in this world and we will never be without suffering here. There is no doubt that the world grows more imperfect all the time. This is why we wait for the revelation of God's glory with such great anticipation and excitement. As deeply as this world has fallen into sin, as powerful as Satan's influence, they cannot compare to the glory of God. All of creation will be set free from sin.

As a Christian you know what the final results will be. You know your destiny which will be revealed. Do you live your life as someone with the promise of the glory of God, or do you allow your sufferings to determine your attitude? Accept your sufferings with patience, knowing that God's glory is so great that it will overshadow all earthly problems. Put the problems of the world in perspective. Deal with your problems with the knowledge of God's promise for you in eternity.

Your destiny is glory. Put your sufferings in their place and live today as one who knows the majesty, mercy, and promises of God.

*"The hope of the wicked perishes with death,
the expectation of the godless is frustrated."*

PROVERBS 11:7

PSALM 56

Verses 10-13

"This I know: that God is on my side.
In God whose word I praise,
In Yahweh, whose word I praise,
In God I put my trust, fearing nothing;
What can man do to me?
I must fulfil the vows I made You, God;
I shall pay You my thank-offerings,
For You have rescued me from Death
To walk in the presence of God
In the light of the living."

MY FOCUS

THE HIGHEST IDEALS

"Never repay evil with evil but let everyone see that you are interested only in the highest ideals."

ROMANS 12:17

Getting even is a very humanistic reaction. Isn't it easy to hurt those that hurt you? Isn't it easy to react negatively when you feel wronged?

This verse spells out what our reactions, actions and thoughts should be. It begins with the word 'never'. Repaying evil for evil is never an option. In these circumstances you are blessed with the opportunity to reveal the love of God, especially to those who have wronged you.

The second keyword is 'see'. Everyone should see that you are interested only in the highest ideals. In order for someone to see, you must do. Your actions will prove where your trust is. This verse calls us to action, promoting only the highest ideals.

The important thing to realize is we are to let others see the love of Christ in every circumstance. We are to react with love to those who hate us. We are to react with kindness to those that offend us. Adverse circumstances give us the perfect opportunity to let others see the high ideals that are spiritual. What a great impact you make when you love those who have mistreated you.

Loving without the thought of getting even keeps you in close identity with God. The evil that others do to you has little impact on you. You are centered in Christ. Let everyone see His grace through your actions and reactions. Keep your eyes on God and keep your interests on His high ideals.

*"A man's attraction lies in his kindness,
better a poor man than a liar."*

PROVERBS 19:22

NO WEAKENING

"That is why there is no weakening on our part, and instead, though this outer man of ours may be falling into decay, the inner man is renewed day by day."

2 CORINTHIANS 4:18

Despite outward appearances and the frailty of our human bodies, there is no weakening in the soul of the believer. It is God's strength that sustains us through illness and injury and His strength that overshadows the daily aches and pains of life. This body may show signs of wear and tear, but this soul continues to mature with His renewal. To come to terms with this confidence requires faith, a faith in something much larger than ourselves. The end of this body is not the end. We can be renewed with energy for Him and His plan for our life every day. Growth and depth of life is fresh and at hand the moment we trust completely in Him. What glorious confidence He provides!

It is difficult in today's society to be content with our aging bodies. We are overwhelmed by messaging that tells us that happiness can only be found in youth. Is there real happiness from the removal of a wrinkle from your face? Is aging something to be avoided at all costs? Why is appearance promoted over substance? The outer man is for today, the inner man is for eternity. It is the inner man that is the recipient of God's peace, happiness, and contentment. It is the inner man that relies on faith, not appearance. It is the inner man whose strength is generated by relationship, not circumstances.

Everyone has their physical challenges from time to time, but those challenges are no match for His strength. The power of God surpasses and makes irrelevant our physical limitations and ailments. The Holy Spirit who dwells inside us puts perspective into our aches and pains. The inner man is imbued by character, morality, faith, and trust. It makes you stronger than any exercise program or diet ever could. It is who we truly are, not some image we try to be that gives us significance. His gift to each of us is the inner strength He has to offer, and He offers it through faith. Stand firm. Stand strong. Let Him provide.

> *"The name of God is a strong tower,*
> *The virtuous man runs to it and is secure."*
>
> **PROVERBS 18:10**

THE GOOD LIFE

"If there are any wise or learned men among you, let them show it by their good lives, with humility and wisdom in their actions."

JAMES 3:13

Knowledge goes hand in hand with humility in the life of a Christian. Compassionate lives have more power than information. It seems like today the goals we set are built around getting more and more information, faster and faster. We want facts as fast as we can get them, not giving enough weight to the context and accuracy. The world speeds up, too often at the expense of wisdom.

Of course we need knowledge, but we also need lives that matter. There has to be time for humility and a place for deep wisdom as we strive to display the good life in Christ. We need to make sure that the condition of our heart keeps up with the information in our head. A life led in the pursuit of mere knowledge is empty if not combined with decisions made by the heart. Real virtue resides in humility and wisdom, not facts and figures. Positions of importance and decisions made by the wise need to be underpinned by the affirmation that the soul is more important than material things. What we know is given power by how we use it.

In this verse James is defining the good life as one that shows itself with humility and wisdom. A humble life puts the concerns and cares of others first. It celebrates the good in others, never demanding attention in return. It gives one the sense and priority of service over self, forgiveness over grudge, and sacrifice over selfishness. It means that you love.

A life lived with wisdom is a life full of compassion. It is a life of application of love, putting real concerns of the heart ahead of all else. It is putting experience, knowledge, and good intentions together to build people up. It uses full context and purpose to find solutions that affect our relationship with God. It means that you love.

> *"When wisdom comes into your heart and knowledge is a delight to you, then prudence will be there to watch over you..."*
>
> **PROVERBS 2:10-11**

NEVER TIRE

"My brothers, never grow tired of doing what is right."

2 THESSALONIANS 3:13

Faith is not a task, it is a part of our character. Believing is not a fleeting emotion, it is a way of life. Doing what is right is not something driven by agenda, it is a commitment to truth and justice. Being a child of God provides the endurance that we need to overcome. Never tire.

We are bombarded day after day with negativity from the world around us. Our "me first" culture, needing immediate gratification, can so easily sap our strength and motivation. Every day we are challenged and every day we are put to the test. It is too often much easier to back away or justify our half-heartedness. We want to compartmentalize our faith, calling on God at our convenience and in our times of need. We let the world have its effect on us, slowly letting our values slip away. For a person of faith, doing what is right needs to be the priority and focus of what we do. Standing firm in our faith, we must keep ethics and morality above anything else. We must always strive for the absolute truth we find in Jesus. Never tire. Much like the early Christians, we today are constantly being presented with new ideas of God and even challenged that there is a God. We struggle when we see a world where sin seems to be taking hold. We get discouraged when we see injustice and evil seem to prevail, while people of faith are marginalized. The Thessalonians were feeling that same kind of pressure, and Paul was doing his best to encourage them in their times of despair. When we read Paul's words, we should be encouraged as well. Never tire.

Let's be honest with ourselves. Our faith life has its ups and downs. We do not always feel the direct hand of God in our hearts. We struggle with our faith and give in to the world. We too often try to use God instead of serve God. Doing what is right does not always come easy or without a price. But we can endure in His love, find peace in His grace, and have a place with Him in His resurrection. We can live with a freedom and assurance because there is absolute power in His name. It may seem like hard work sometimes, but we must never tire.

With God on our side, we will never lose. With God on our side, we find and appreciate the dignity of every life. With God on our side, victory is ours. We stand on the right side of things because we believe in a God that is loving and powerful, just and true, graceful and present. Doing what is right is our way of showing to whom we belong and in whom we believe. Take heart and live with the confidence and principle that God's love provides. We are in a marathon relationship with God, and our eternity is determined through faith. His strength will carry us through, and His love will help us endure. Never tire.

> *"Then you will understand what virtue is, justice, and fair dealing, all paths that lead to happiness."*
>
> **PROVERBS 2:9**

IT IS ABOUT FAITH

> *"Though we were born Jews and not pagan sinners, we acknowledge that what makes a man righteous is not obedience to the Law, but faith in Jesus Christ. We had to become believers in Christ Jesus no less than you had, and now we hold that faith in Christ rather than fidelity to the Law is what justifies us, and that no one can be justified by keeping the Law."*
>
> GALATIANS 2:15-16

It is not about what you do, it is about who He is. The human struggle that Paul is talking about is just as prevalent today as it was in the early church. All of us struggle with the perception that if I could just be a little better, if I am just a nice person, or if I try to be good, I will be saved in the end. As we try to perfect ourselves, we lose sight of the saving grace of the Perfect One, Jesus Christ. In these verses Paul puts into the most direct words that it is faith that makes the difference. It is faith in Christ's suffering, death, and resurrection that justifies us. Period.

Then, like now, we struggle with putting our full reliance on this concept. We fail to recognize that we cannot meet the requirements of the Law on our own, and no amount of self-righteous behavior will change that fact. Being a good person does not save you. Doing your best does not save you. Being religious does not save you. Faith in the redemptive grace of God and the atoning sacrifice of Christ saves. Period. Paul was so adamant about these facts because the converts of the time were placing their dependence on outward signs and rituals instead of the saving grace of Christ. The emphasis was on personal acts instead of Christ. They felt that ritual would set you apart as a requirement to be saved. But Paul lets it be known that Christ died for all, and the gift of salvation was available to all through faith. There is only one requirement to be saved and that is faith.

It is not about what you do, it is about who He is. It is about what He does for us through grace. It is about our response in faith to that grace as we live our lives dedicated to Christ. The saving justification that Christ provides is right in front of us. We can live free, acknowledging but not subject to the Law. Christ has done the work for each of us. May our faith in Christ be the foundation for our lives.

> *"Trust wholeheartedly in God,*
> *Put no faith in your own perception."*
>
> PROVERBS 3:5

FIND CONTENTMENT

"Keep your lives free from the love of money and be content with what you have, because God has said; Never will I leave you, never will I forsake you."

HEBREWS 13:5

How much is enough? The answer to this question for most of us cannot be answered easily. The answer is usually, "just a little more than what I have." We strive so hard for more that we overlook what we have, what God has blessed us with. God's promise is that He will not forsake us. God will provide for our needs. The problem comes when we can't tell the difference between needs and wants. Our selfishness convinces us that our wants are really necessary for our happiness.

Contentment is a virtue. God has placed us where He wants us to be for His purpose. How disrespectful it is to tell God that we want more gifts than He has provided. The love of money places our selfishness at the center of our being, supplanting the grace of God from its rightful perch. Our hardened heart leaves little space for God to dwell. Our continual pursuit of more distrusts God's promises. This passage and its promises should give us peace and contentment, knowing and trusting that God is someone we can depend on.

FOCUS

What is your focus? Does the love of money dominate your efforts? Does the love of money determine your actions and the way you treat others? Money itself is not evil, but the love of money is. Be content with what you have. Your contentment will allow a place for God in your heart. Your actions and focus will be changed when you accept and rely on the promises of God. How blessed we are!!! God will not forsake us, He will never leave.

Replace your pursuit of money with the pursuit of knowing and trusting God. Contentment and peace will surely follow.

> *"He who trusts in riches will have his fall,*
> *the virtuous will flourish like the leaves."*

PROVERBS 11:28

PSALM 106

Verses 1-2

"Alleluia!
Give thanks to God, for He is good,
His love is everlasting!
Who can count all God's triumphs?
Who can praise Him enough?"

MY FOCUS

THE GOOD SHEPHERD

"I am the good shepherd; I know My own and My own know Me."

JOHN 10:14

Jesus is the good shepherd, the one who cares for our souls and leads us down the right path. To all who believe, His voice makes us secure in the knowledge that we are in the hands of someone who loves us. He nurtures us and guides us where we need to go. He protects and secures us in His commitment to our safety. He is always present, always involved, and always loving. He is the Good Shepherd.

Jesus knows us inside and out. He knows our hearts and our minds. He knows our motivations and our commitment. He knows our challenges and weaknesses. He is the Good Shepherd. He alone is the pure essence of where we can find rest. We are known completely only by Him. What a blessing it is to be known individually by Jesus. We are never alone. His care for us never fails. We are never unloved.

When we really know Jesus, we experience His peace and love. Knowing about Jesus is much different than knowing the real Jesus. When we know Him we trust, we obey, we surrender. When we know Him we find rest, peace, and security in His arms. When we know Him we live free to love abundantly. When we know Him we let His power reign, His supremacy lead, and His majesty overwhelm. When we really know Jesus we let His deity lead us as we trust Him completely. He is the good shepherd. Hear His voice. Follow His lead. Obey His commands. Rest in the warm embrace of Jesus.

> *"The fear of God leads to life,*
> *A man has food and shelter, and no evil to fear."*
>
> PROVERBS 19:23

ENDURE

"Your endurance will win you your lives."

LUKE 21:19

Sometimes we can drive ourselves crazy looking for solutions to our problems. Our anxiety can overwhelm us when things do not line up exactly as we want. When all we see is injustice and unfairness, we let it eat at us. Sometimes the only answer is to endure. Sometimes all we are asked to do is to stay firm in our beliefs as the world whirls around us. We are to rely on God, always, and continue on our path towards Him. It is in His strength we can stay the course towards righteousness. We can endure anything with Him.

Things can be so frustrating when we feel powerless to change the environment around us. We are constantly under pressure to bend to the current politically correct posture or socially acceptable position, challenging us to stay true to the Word and true to God. If we continue to always stand on the firm foundation of Christ, we can endure whatever comes our way with hope, surety, and joy. Too often we are afraid of what the world has presented to us and forget that God is stronger and has power over everything. Despite our fears of failure we can rest in the knowledge that God will never fail us. We can endure because of His strength, His promises, and His grace. Stand firm and never give up. He will see us through. Through our faith in Him we can sustain against any enemy, maintain our trust and reliance on Him, and hold fast to the absolute truth of His grace. Through faith we can live a life of action, not reaction, based on His love and His righteousness. Through faith we can find rest and security in a world that offers neither. Through faith we can endure…anything.

Times change, but God doesn't. Attitudes change, but God doesn't. Expectations change, but God doesn't. We are called to endure, holding on tightly to God and not letting Him go. Our worth and value is not based on this world, it is based on our willingness to hold on tightly to Him. It is based on our desire to see our life in Christ to its earthly completion, never surrendering and never unwavering. We have His promise of eternity waiting for us. In Him, we can endure.

> *"The human spirit can endure in sickness,*
> *but a crushed spirit who can bear?"*
>
> **PROVERBS 18:14 NIV**

THE FULL ARMOR

"Put on the full armor of God so that you can take your stand against the devil's schemes."

EPHESIANS 6:11

God has enough armor to protect us in every circumstance. But to put on the full armor we have to be committed without reservation. Too many of us think we can prevail with only certain pieces of the armor, but the devil is attacking at full force. All of God's armor is required to outlast the slings of the enemy. Usually we wait for a problem, some physical need to be protected, and then we will arm ourselves with what is necessary for the occasion. This is not what we are told to do!

To withstand the devil's schemes requires full armor, every day and in all circumstances. The devil's schemes are beyond our mortal abilities to defend ourselves. We have to have daily accounting of our armor. We must recognize our weak spots and pray for God's armor to protect us. You know your weaknesses and so does God and so does the devil. So do something about it!

Put on God's armor and prepare yourself for battle. How blessed we are that we know God's armor will withstand the devil's schemes. Be prepared! Don't sacrifice one area of protection to serve another.

Be protected by God from head to toe. Act like a Christian. Speak like a Christian. Love like a Christian. Protect your soul as well as your body. Encase yourself within God and let His power protect you. Then, you can live with confidence.

Do you wear the full armor of God? Are you wearing it now? Do your actions show the full confidence of God's protection? Actively hold on to the promises of God and wear them in your daily battles. Trust the protection and depend on it. Put your faith in God and deny the devil any opportunities. Live today with the confidence of one protected and saved through the grace of God.

"Uprightness stands guard over one whose way is honest,
sin causes the ruin of the wicked."

PROVERBS 13:6

MODEL YOURSELF

"Do not model yourselves on the behavior of the world around you, but let your behavior change, modeled by your new mind. This is the only way to discover the will of God and know what is good, what it is that God wants, what is the perfect thing to do."

ROMANS 12:2

How much influence do you let the world have over you? This verse reminds us of three important goals that we should all have and also gives us the answer to obtaining these goals. We need to know what is good. We need to know what God wants. And we need to know the perfect thing to do.

The world around us will never give us the answers to these important questions. In fact, the world turns us away from our goals as Christians, substituting instead a model of living far from the desires of God. We must let our behaviors change, modeled by our new mind. The world is not in charge of your behavior. Too often we use this world as our reference in how to live our lives. The problem is that the world is full of sin. Do not let your life be modeled on sin!

Instead, we are called to be models of life under the direction of God's will. The will of God is revealed in the knowledge of Him, not of this world. The world does not show us what God wants. Only through a close relationship with Him can we know what God wants. The perfect thing to do will never be shown by this world, but only through trust in God. Perfection lies only with God.

Our challenge is clear. How do we live in the world while identifying with God? Without a change of behavior and a desire to know the will of God we cannot reach our three goals. God will reveal Himself when we act according to the new mind God gives us. The world is not our measuring stick. Your new mind, your new trust, your new motives, and your changed behavior will allow these three important goals to be obtained. With this new behavior comes peace of mind and a closeness to God based on trust, reliance, and obedience. Let your behavior display to the world who is your model. Let God be revealed through you.

> *"Men of depraved heart are abhorrent to God,
> dear to him, those whose ways are blameless."*
>
> PROVERBS 11:20

DECLARE YOURSELF

"So if anyone declares himself for Me in the presence of men, I will declare Myself for him in the presence of My Father in heaven."

MATTHEW 10:32

In your daily life, in the presence of men, does your life declare yourself for Christ? Your declaration is not an oral statement, but a visible means of living. There should be no mystery as to whether or not your life declares itself for Christ. The character and actions of your life shouts some type of declaration. The question is, for whom do you declare? Our society urges us to shout for ourselves. How much do you have? How much do you want? The piling up of material things will bring you happiness. These are the lies of the world.

Where is the declaration for Christ? What value is put on kindness, humility, thoughtfulness, and servanthood? When is sacrifice and obedience honored instead of power, prestige, and wealth? The things of God are not of this world. Let your life declare its foundation and direction. A sympathetic and generous heart to those in need declares yourself to Him. Humility and servanthood declare yourself to Him. Loving family relationships and the honoring of your parents declares yourself to Him. Honesty and a truthful tongue declare yourself to Him. Obedience to the Word of God declares yourself to Him. Your declaration speaks louder from your heart and actions than by your mouth. Christ knows your heart and your motivations. Men will see your declarations through your attitude, priorities, and actions.

We are blessed with the peace of our Savior who will declare you His own to the Father. What He asks is that we let our entire lives declare Him, illuminating a darkened world with His truth and power. We play an important role in keeping Christ alive before the world of men. It is your active declaration that continues to reveal your faith in the truth of Christ. Your declaration keeps Christ alive in you and lets His power work through you. Christ wants to declare you for Himself. Live more than a Christian life, live with Christ in you. Declare Him openly with your life.

"God stands far from the wicked,
But He listens to the prayers of the virtuous."

PROVERBS 15:29

THE LIGHT

"I, the light, have come into the world, so that whoever believes in Me need not stay in the dark anymore."

JOHN 12:46

What images do you have when you think about darkness? Some of the words used in the dictionary are: loneliness, fear, tragedy, evil, wicked, gloomy, hidden, secret, immoral, and secretive. These are almost exclusively words with negative connotations. These words paint a picture of desperation and despair.

What images do you have when you think about light? Some of the words used in the dictionary are: illumination, enlightenment, truth, gentleness, something that makes seeing possible. The list is full of positive thoughts. These words paint a picture of hope and possibility. Sin is darkness. Christ is light. Sin hides the truth while Christ reveals it. Sin impedes while Christ nurtures. Sin diminishes while Christ flourishes. Sin steals your soul while Christ empowers it. Sin is powerful but Christ is always more powerful. Darkness will always have to give way to light. Always. Christ is often referred to as the Light which has come to overpower the darkness of the world. There is hope and brightness in the Light. There is knowledge and awareness in the Light. There is direction and safety in the Light. Is the Light shining in your life?

The darkness of sadness and remorse can be overcome through the light of Christ. The shadows of fear and loneliness can disappear when the light of Christ shines brightly. The darkness in our hearts can be captured with a heart filled with Christ. This verse is a reminder and assurance of the power of the light of Christ. He overcame so you can overcome. He shines so that you may reflect. He is, and always will be, victorious over any darkness. He came to us, illuminating both our hearts and minds so that we can live a life full of light and hope. With Christ, we are no longer subject to the darkness. Darkness cannot control us because of the power in His light. Through faith the Light is ours, a free gift that will shine forever. How blessed we are. How powerful God is. He is the source, the provider, and the character of light. Let it shine.

> *"The light of virtuous men burns bright,*
> *The lamp of the wicked goes out."*
>
> PROVERBS 13:9

PSALM 27

Verses 4-5

"One thing I ask of God,
One thing I seek:
To live in the house of God
All the days of my life,
To enjoy the sweetness of God
And to consult Him in His Temple.
For He shelters me under His awning,
In times of trouble;
He hides me deep in His tent,
Sets me high on a rock."

MY FOCUS

GOOD PURPOSE

"The particular way in which the Spirit is given to each person is for a good purpose."

1 CORINTHIANS 12:7

Each of us is a unique creation of God. We were not meant to be the same and were not meant for the same purposes. We were meant to complement each other with our commitment to follow the Spirit where and how it leads. Every created creature is of special value to God, and His love for each of us knows no bounds. None is greater. None is less important. All are loved.

I firmly believe that God places us where we are for His particular reason. We are gifted with certain talents and assets for His particular reason. We have a particular purpose in life, even if at times we do not recognize it. God has fashioned us individually. God has purpose, and that purpose is always for good. We are not aimlessly passing time on this planet merely the result of random things coming together by chance. We have influence and presence, opportunity and responsibility, and obligation and purpose. The Spirit that dwells inside of us gives us guidance and direction as God's ultimate plan works out.

It is so easy to wait for inspiration to strike by way of some individual or event. The truth is you are already inspired by the Spirit working within you. You have the exact talents that God desires you to have. God's timing is always perfect. He will use the Spirit within you for good purpose for His plan. Will you be used today to meet the needs of someone else? Will you be the answer to someone's prayer today? Will you be moved to comfort and show compassion to just the right person at just the right time? Our function is to be ready to be used by the Spirit at all times. We may never know the impact that we can have when we let the Spirit determine our purpose at any particular time. Our joy and hope come from the fact that God's plan is a perfect plan and His plan includes us.

Human nature would have us comparing ourselves to others. We are led to question whether we are competent enough, talented enough, or smart enough. We doubt ourselves and our abilities. But this verse assures us that whatever you are blessed with is exactly what you are supposed to be blessed with. You and your faith are needed and an important part of the plan of God. You have purpose, value, and worth in the eyes of God. Recognize that you are a different and unique creation, endowed with the Spirit for GOOD purpose. We should never underestimate or undervalue how God created us or our capacity to be used for His good purpose.

A preacher needs a listener. An orator needs an audience. A caregiver needs a patient. A parent needs a child. A writer needs a reader. Everyone needs to be loved. There is a place for all of us, a divine purpose. There is a powerful Spirit within each of us giving us exactly what we need when we need it. Thank God for your place in His plan and for the Spirit who guides you. There is only one you, and that is the way God intended it to be.

"Plans multiply in the human heart,
But the purpose of God stands firm."

PROVERBS 19:21

THE SOLID BASE OF FAITH

"...as long as you persevere and stand firm on the solid base of faith, never letting yourself drift away from the hope promised by the Good News, which you have heard, which has been preached to the whole human race, and of which I, Paul, have become the servant."

COLOSSIANS 1:23

What we believe and how we practice that belief are the means by which we develop our integrity and our character. It is the dedication and commitment to that belief that solidifies the consistency of our heart. Where we stand determines our attitudes, action, peace, and contentment. If we value our belief, we are able to persevere even through the challenges we face day after day, moment by moment. When we invest our full selves in something, we need to know that it is worth the battle and something we can trust in. Christ is the foundation that never fails.

Even in the face of difficulty, stand on the solid base of faith. When difficult choices need to be made, stand on the solid base of faith. When we are disappointed and feel depressed, know that the solid base of faith will support you. When the world around us seems to be overcome with turmoil, feel the peace of the victory of Christ in the solid base of faith. When you celebrate, give praise and thanksgiving because of your solid base of faith.

What we believe determines who we are. Faith in Christ determines to whom we belong. Stand firm on the solid base that never changes and always gives hope.

Spiritual drift is a constant threat. When we do not prioritize and focus on the most important things it is easy to lose sight. It is easy to compromise or rationalize our way into devaluing some of the most important things. Each small step away from the truth eventually leads us further from what we know is right. It is easy to slip. Only by consistent commitment to holding fast, standing firm, and keeping focus on our faith in Christ can we keep our hope in the Good News alive and active.

There are more and more things that compete for attention. Outside influences come at us faster and faster. It is ever more difficult to determine what truth is as competing opinions and points of view try to influence our minds. Our challenge is to remember, at all times, that there is but one real, absolute truth. His name is Jesus. His truth is love. His truth never fails. His truth is complete and uncompromising. In Him and Him alone we must place our faith. He and He alone is the solid base. Only through Him are we saved. He is the strong tower where we can find His protection, peace, power, and grace. Stand firm. Stand strong.

> *"When the storm is over, the wicked man is no more,*
> *But the virtuous stands firm forever."*

PROVERBS 10:25

GO TO HIM

"Come to me, all you who labor and are overburdened and I will give you rest."

MATTHEW 11:28

Christ came to free us. Only in Him can we find true peace. He came to unburden us from the futility of ourselves. Too often we want to create our own salvation, only to find that through our own labors we cannot obtain our goal. We set ourselves up for failure and frustration time and time again. The yield of such labors leaves us with feelings of inadequacy and guilt. We constantly search for contentment and peace, but find ourselves struggling with our lack of control and dependence on those things that are not eternal.

It is time to face the facts! Left to our own perceptions of happiness and contentment, we will continue to fall short. We will continue to fall victim to the temptations that surround us. Our pride and ego lead us down a path of selfishness. So where can we get our rest? Who has a plan for our eternal welfare? Where shall we go? The offer to find our rest is simple. "Come to me." God is there for us, offering us the salvation we desire freely. What we cannot obtain on our own He holds out to us as a gift. The peace that we struggle to find awaits each of us, if we will only come. This verse is one that gives us a glimpse of the character of Christ. He cares so deeply for all those who toil through everyday circumstances and gives us His enduring promise of hope. The best answer, the only answer, lies in Him and not in us. In Him is the hope to find peace and security. In Him we can trust to provide us with a contentment that surpasses our understanding. All He asks is that we come. His forgiving nature and inclusive promise provide us with a security we cannot obtain on our own.

None of our work is in vain when we toil for His purposes. He comforts and consoles. He wipes away the temporary tear and promises us eternal rest. So what is stopping us from turning our burdens over to Him? What is stopping us from taking the steps to Him? Let the desire to control our lives be swallowed up by His promises. Don't wait any longer. He is waiting. GO!

> *"Deceit is in the heart of the schemer,*
> *joy with those who give counsels of peace."*
>
> **PROVERBS 12:20**

THE FORTITUDE OF CHRIST

"May the Lord turn your hearts towards the love of God and the fortitude of Christ."

2 THESSALONIANS 3:5

When we rely on Christ, we are the beneficiaries of His attributes of strength, courage, and fortitude. His strength allows us to persevere in times of trial and be bold in times of challenge. His strength allows us to endure adversity with a sense of courage and surety. His strength allows us to resist those who attack us and stand firm in times of conflict. It is through His power that we can confront danger, temptation, and the unknown. A firm conviction and trust in our living God will embolden our spirits. His strength. His fortitude.

The suffering, death, and resurrection of Christ is the greatest example of the love of God for the world. The sacrifice of Christ changed our past, present, and future in an act of love toward all mankind. God's grace changes everything. His grace gives us a reason to turn our hearts toward Him as we honor and obey, receiving credit for His atoning blood. He loved us first, putting His love on display for everyone to see and everyone to experience. A heart turned toward the love of God is a heart that reflects the light of truth that He proclaims through grace. A heart full of faith sees the world through the lens of Christ, recognizing the power and majesty of God and His love.

There is no doubt that we struggle in this world at times, and we find it hard to find the strength to endure. There is no need to go alone! His love has already won the battle for us. The fortitude of Christ will see us through. With a heart turned towards God we can be bold in our motivations to love both our God and our fellow man with abundance and compassion. With the fortitude of Christ we can endure anything, stand firm in difficult situations, and experience His truth and His grace. With the love of Christ standing firmly by our side we can find peace, fulfillment, and rest. His love becomes our fortress. His fortitude.

"To be afraid of men is a snare,
He who puts his trust in God is secure."

PROVERBS 29:25

RELY ON THE POWER OF GOD

*"...bear the hardships for the sake of the Good News,
relying on the power of God who has saved us and called us to be
holy—not because of anything we ourselves have done
but for His own purpose and by His own grace."*

2 TIMOTHY 1:8-9

Hardships may occur as a direct result of our work for the Lord. These fleeting troubles can be endured by relying on the power of God. God's plan for us is much broader than we can comprehend. God's purpose cannot always be discerned by us. It is in our nature to avoid hardships or to overcome them by ourselves.

This verse clearly tells us that nothing that we have done by ourselves can make us holy. It is only through the power of God and His grace that we are saved souls. This verse also tells us that there will be hardships for the sake of the Good News. We shouldn't be surprised when these hardships come, but instead know that these hardships should serve to strengthen our reliance on the power of God. Surely God will see us through our hardships for His own purpose and grace.

It is not our job to attempt to figure out why times are difficult. We are to bear the hardships. Paul writes this letter to Timothy while in prison, secure in his complete faith in the power of God that he will be able to bear his circumstances. His acknowledgment that only by God's grace are we called to be holy while enduring his hardships serves as an invaluable example to us. Do you acknowledge that God has His own purpose for you? Are you willing to bear the hardships for the sake of the Good News?

This verse should serve to encourage us to be unashamed of our reliance on God and give us the knowledge that we will overcome any hardship that ensues because we rely fully on the power of God. What great confidence this should give us! Be unafraid! Work boldly for the sake of the Good News. You have the assurance that you can bear all your hardships. Let God use you for His own purpose with confidence and faith.

> *"God made everything for its own purpose,*
> *yes, even the wicked for the day of disaster."*

PROVERBS 16:4

BE BRAVE

*"Be awake to all the danger; stay firm in the faith;
be brave and be strong."*

1 CORINTHIANS 16:13

This is our call to action! Through faith in Christ we are the protectors of the gifts which we have been given. Through faith we have the courage and bravery necessary to take on the world. Through faith we have sufficient strength to stand against every enemy. Be on guard! Be ready! Be strong!

It is very easy to turn a blind eye to all the perils that surround us. It is much easier to take the path of least resistance, avoiding the risks that come with standing for the principles of Jesus. Those of us that do not like conflict shy away from situations that might bring contradiction or controversy to the forefront. We find it much easier to compromise and rationalize instead of standing firmly on the foundation of Christ. We become so used to a secular world that pushes God away that we forget our obligation as people of faith to put our focus on Christ in all situations. There is danger in our neglect and harm in our blindness. Be awake!

Faith in Christ is the foundation of everything. It is through this lens that we must focus our behaviors, attitudes, and actions. Without faith we are lost and without principle. With faith we are confident and assured. Without faith we are alone and on our own. With faith we are covered by the blood of Christ. We are welcomed into His eternal family. Without faith we merely exist. With faith we live richly, free to love abundantly. Stand firm in the faith!

It is not easy to stand firmly in a world that wants to exclude and minimize our faith. We cannot back down when challenged or turn our backs on our values. A world that wants to set its own rules and morality needs to be confronted strongly with the values of Christ. Being brave in these situations means that the values we protect are worth fighting and standing for. Being strong includes service and sacrifice. It means that truth and honesty will always win out. It means integrity will always supersede selfishness and pride in Jesus will overshadow pride in anything else. It means finding the best in people, shunning the temptation to tear down anyone. It means to be just and fair to everyone.

We are able to be brave and strong because the victory has already been won. We are on the winning side when we have Jesus. Our eternity is secure and our peace is at hand when we have Jesus. Be proud of the faith that resides within you and let that confidence in Him shine to all those around you. Speak His truth and live His truth. Love.

"If you lose heart, when adversity comes your strength will only be weakness."

PROVERBS 24:10

PSALM 67

Verses 1-4

"May God show kindness and bless us,
And make His face smile on us!
For then the earth will acknowledge Your ways
And all the nations will know of Your power to save.
Let the nations praise You, O God,
Let all the nations praise You!
Let the nations shout and sing for joy,
Since You dispense true justice to the world;
You dispense strict justice to the peoples,
On earth You rule the nations."

MY FOCUS

FAITH AND GOOD WORKS

"Faith is like that: if good works do not go with it, it is quite dead."

JAMES 2:17

What good is faith if it doesn't change our behavior? Real faith shapes our motivations, priorities, and actions. When we have faith in Christ, our aspirations and goals change.

What do your works reveal about your faith? Who do you depend on, God or yourself? So many of us want to make faith an intellectual or emotional exercise. We want to think our way to heaven or get a good feeling about ourselves because we have good intentions. This verse could not be any clearer. Good works are to be performed and are the result of our faith. Good works are the active expression of our obedience and commitment to a life of Christian humility and purpose. Good works are a visible means of testifying to our relationship with God. They are a confirmation that God is in charge, and an acknowledgment of our Christian duties.

If you want to call yourself a Christian, then act like it! Our Christian response to every type of situation that God puts us in demonstrates our trust in Him. If you confess your faith with your words, then demonstrate that faith with your works. Faith is a commitment that determines our response, action, compassion, and priorities in every situation.

You can do good works every day. Opportunities to put your faith into action are never far away. The manner in which you interact with those around you, the way you handle adversity, and the way that you are willing to help others reveal your faith. The acknowledgment that all gifts come from God, your stewardship of those gifts, and the praise and glory that you give God reveal who you trust. Your sacrificial attitude, peaceful heart, and inward joy reveal your reliance on God.

God's promises are real. The Holy Spirit that dwells in your heart is real, too. We are saved by faith, not by works. True faith will lead to a life full of good works. Faith without good works is of no benefit. Good works without faith are hollow. Faith requires action. That action and your motivations will be pure when based on your faith. Your life of faith-based good works will be a living example of how real and alive God is. Keep your faith alive!

> *"Let kindliness and loyalty never leave you,*
> *Tie them around your neck,*
> *Write them on the tablet of your heart."*

PROVERBS 3:3

DO MORE THAN LISTEN

*"It is not listening to the Law but keeping it
that will make people holy in the sight of God."*

ROMANS 2:13

The proof of your character is not what you know, but what you do. How do you put your faith into action? It is action that makes your faith and commitment come alive, allowing God to use you to affect the world around you. It is also by your actions that those around you judge the level of your commitment and the depth of your dedication. It is by your actions that those in the world see a glimpse of how God works in the lives of believers. It is by your actions that you witness to the power, patience, and grace of the Almighty God.

Knowing what is right is not enough, but it is an important part in directing your actions. Our actions need to be pure and well-intentioned, but more importantly, be based on God's laws. It is choosing the right path and following God's will in your life that pleases God. Do you have the courage to do what you know is right? It isn't always easy nor should you expect it to be. The temptation to take the easy way and accept secular concepts is ever- present. Too often we let secular norms cloud our judgment and we rationalize our behavior to a level much less than what God demands.

How committed are you? Can you put your faith into action? There is a big difference between hearing the truth and living committed to it. Living the faith keeps your commitment at the forefront, constantly allowing you to make decisions that confirm your devotion. Living the truth keeps your faith growing, alive, and real. Living the truth adds awareness and obedience to your character.

God expects our commitment to be complete and much more than just an intellectual endeavor. He wants the complete person, willing to live completely in Him. May we all keep God's laws alive by keeping them and making them part of all decisions and situations. Listen, believe it, and live it.

> *"And now, my sons, listen to me; Listen to instruction and learn to be wise, Do not ignore it. Happy those who keep my ways."*
>
> PROVERBS 8:32

BROTHERHOOD

"These remained faithful to the teaching of the apostles, to the brotherhood, to the breaking of bread and to the prayers."

ACTS 2:42

The early believers in Christ set a good example for us all to follow. They prioritized godly things. They met the needs of their fellow believers. They knew to be thankful for having their own needs met. And most of all, they sought a close relationship with God. Theirs was truly a brotherhood.

They understood each other as people longing for and believing in the Messiah. They had common problems and common concerns. They felt a common bond as they had heard and seen Jesus in action and believed wholeheartedly the apostles who led them. They were bound together by belief in Jesus and supported each other in every way that they could. Their brotherhood was pure in its beliefs and its motives. They were a brotherhood sustained by the reality of Jesus. Are you part of a brotherhood with the same excitement and commitment?

We usually find commonality among those we call friends. Is that common ground Jesus? The early believers were immersed in their commitment, willing to sacrifice for the good of their fellow believers. They were willing to be obedient and willing to put their love on display. They shared what they had, intended only the best for each other, and found strength in their commitment to Jesus. We could all use that kind of brotherhood.

Most importantly they prayed. They knew that relationship with God would sustain them through any hardship and that God was worthy of their prayer. Christ was real. Christ was a conqueror. Christ was the Messiah. Christ was their salvation. As you search your heart, let Christ be the head of your brotherhood and the source of peace in your life. Show compassion wherever you can and be bonded to Christ with His grace and love. As we care for others we show His care for us.

> *"A friend is a friend at all times,*
> *It is for adversity that a brother is born."*

PROVERBS 17:17

HOW TO TREAT TRIALS

"My brothers, you will always have your trials but, when they come, try to treat them as a happy privilege; you understand that your faith is only put to the test to make you patient, but patience too is to have its practical results so that you will become fully developed, complete, with nothing missing."

JAMES 1:2-4

How different would your daily attitude be if you looked at all your trials as a happy privilege? Wouldn't we handle our trials differently if we looked at them as a chance to further develop our character?

Notice that this verse does not say 'persevere through your trials'. It says we are to look upon these trials as a happy privilege. What a change this outlook would bring! Perhaps what we consider problems might not be problems at all if we consider them a happy privilege.

We are blessed with trials to develop patience. Everyone is faced with trials, but the challenge for the Christian is to keep a different perspective about those trials. Trials come before us to test our faith. Do you really trust God to see you through your trials, or do you put your faith in your own ability to find your way? Do you have the patience to allow God to work in your life, or do you search for quick answers? Your trials can only be treated as happy privilege if you place your full trust in God.

We may not understand or like the trials put before us. But if we realize and believe that all our trials are put before us to see who we really trust, we can stand firm and say thank you to God for continuing to build us. We want to be mature Christians. This can only be accomplished if we are challenged to put our faith into action in daily circumstances. The patience that we display fortifies our reliance on God, not ourselves. Nothing can speak louder for God than a happy Christian, one who is happy in all circumstances and under any trial. When you put your faith into action you no longer have to fear your trials.

> *"The wicked do not know what justice means,*
> *those who fear God understand everything."*
>
> **PROVERBS 28:5**

RELATIONSHIPS

"Wives, give way to your husbands, as you should in the Lord. Husbands love your wives and treat them with gentleness. Children, be obedient to your parents always, because that is that will please the Lord. Parents, never drive your children to resentment or you will make them feel frustrated."

COLOSSIANS 3:18-21

Relationships come in many forms and each carries responsibilities. Healthy relationships all have a common thread that holds them together. That thread is the Lord.

This verse talks about two types of relationships, husbands and wives, and parents and children. A breakdown in any of these relationships will have an adverse effect on the other. Does the picture of godly relationships described in this text mirror your own? Relationships are fueled by emotions. Respect, honor, gentleness, concern, and love are words that describe someone's heart. The relationships described in Colossians are all based on and anchored on the intimate relationship that God has with His people. The boundless love of God and His desire to have a relationship with us should shine before us as a testament to the importance that God puts on relationships.

Every one of the commands in these verses can be seen in action by the love of God. God sacrificed for us. God is gentle towards us. God is consistent with us. God's love for us is complete. His willingness to sacrifice for us in order to nurture our relationships together should be a model for all our family relationships.

The gentleness with which a husband treats his wife identifies him as a man willing to sacrifice for her. The respect that a wife shows her husband identifies her as a woman willing to sacrifice. Children who are willing to listen and obey their parents out of respect show that they are willing to give some things up and sacrifice. Parents whose goals are to nurture the development of their children and take the time to guide their experiences show that they are willing to sacrifice for their children.

God does not want us to merely call ourselves Christians; He wants a relationship with you. Husbands should do all they can to enrich their relationships with their wives and help her thrive. Wives should find a way to encourage and empower their husbands to be effective leaders. Parents have the awesome responsibility to see to it that their children understand the importance of fruitful relationships. Frustrated children can tear down relationships. Be sure that all your decisions with your children are driven by the type of love that God consistently shows us. Children owe much to their parents, just as we as adults owe much to God. Obedience should be our response.

Commitment, sacrifice, concern. These traits should be in action toward all you love around you. Don't just build friendships or acquaintances. Build impactful relationships. All of the components needed to build relationships are revealed in God. Open yourself to God for a deep relationship with him. Open yourself to the relationships with those around you. Nothing can be more fulfilling than relationships. Embrace them.

> *"Correct your son, and he will give you peace of mind;*
> *he will delight your soul."*
>
> PROVERBS 29:17

EVEN IF

"Nothing therefore can come between us and the love of Christ, even if we are troubled or worried, or being persecuted, or lacking food or clothes, or being threatened or even attacked."

ROMANS 8:35

In times of uncertainty, turmoil, and fear there is one constant that can be depended upon 100% of the time: the love of Christ. There is no barrier that is too high for His love. There is no difficulty too immense to overshadow the connection between us and His love. Despite our cares and worries, despite us being preoccupied by our circumstances, and despite feeling vulnerable and at risk, we can rest assured that the love of Christ is always there. In His love we can find His peace.

Life is a perpetual stream of barriers. There are roadblocks and obstacles in our daily lives that can get in the way of our realizing the love of Christ. Christ knew firsthand the trials and tribulations we would face here on earth, yet He never stopped living in pure love. He ministered to people daily who were anxious about their circumstances, looking for someone to ease their discomfort and disease. He saw the faces of those who worried about surviving in a harsh world that did not care about the poor and needy. And He loved. There were no paybacks expected and no social barriers to overcome. He simply loved with no thought of compensation. He set no requirements and left no one out. He was love.

It is easy to ask, "where is God" when we are in difficult times and see pain and suffering around us. It is easy to feel distance from God when life has let us down. It is easy to care so much about ourselves that we lose sight of God. But He is here now. He is here always. So whatever your "even if" is, "even if" we worry and have doubts, and "even if" we feel separated, Christ loves you beyond any of them. His love is for each of us and it is intimate, full, unconditional, and within our reach. His love is there, close and ours for the believing. We have so many things that we give power to in our lives that sometimes we build a wall between ourselves and God. Our anxieties and worries can push God aside and we lose focus on eternity and look only to the immediate. God puts up no such barriers. How comforting it is to know that in all circumstances we can know that we are always loved. Let the power of His love thrive in whatever situation you find yourself. Rest in the knowledge that nothing prevents you from accessing His love. Turn your "even if" into a "rest assured." He is love.

"If you lose heart, when adversity comes your strength will only be weakness."

PROVERBS 24:10

PSALM 71

Verses 1-4

"In You, God, I take shelter; never let me be disgraced.
In Your righteousness rescue me, deliver me,
    Turn Your ear to me and save me!
    Be a sheltering rock for me,
    A walled fortress to save me!
For You are my rock, my fortress.
My God, rescue me from the hands of the wicked,
    From the clutches of rogue and tyrant!"

MY FOCUS

GIVE OF YOURSELVES

"He replied, 'Give them something to eat yourselves.'"

MARK 6:37

When the disciples of Jesus looked out over the crowd of 5,000 who were hungry, they looked to Jesus for a resolution to the problem. The crowd needed to be fed. Jesus knew they needed to be fed with both food for their bodies and food for their souls. Jesus could have taken away the hunger pangs or fed them Himself, but He let the disciples be part of the miracle. The disciples were looking for an external solution when what was needed was an internal confidence and trust in Jesus. How often do we look for a miracle from afar instead of trusting God enough to let us be part of His work? How differently would you go about your day if you had an attitude that you personally were going to be used by God to be the answer to someone's prayer? Be ready…be aware…allow yourself to be ready to give.

Jesus needed those 5,000 fed to hear Him. The 5,000 needed to be fed so they could experience the presence of the Lord. The compassion of Jesus was made available to the multitude who were being served by the disciples. The crowd was fed with both food and the Spirit as the disciples were used in the miracle. Are you ready to be used today? Are you ready to set the stage for others to feel and experience the compassion of Jesus?

What seemed impossible to the disciples became reality in an instant. At first they were overwhelmed by the magnitude of Jesus' command, wondering how they could possibly feed so many. Then they did the most important thing; they listened and obeyed. It probably made no sense to them, yet they did exactly what Jesus asked them to do. They did not let the size of the challenge deter them from simply doing what Jesus asked…and the miracle happened. They were willing to be used as servants for the purposes of Jesus and the benefit of many. Are you ready to be used?

It may only be five loaves and two fish, but in the hands of Jesus it can multiply beyond any expectations. You may feel you do not have much to give, but in the hands of Jesus, you can have influence beyond anything you can imagine. Obstacles may seem insurmountable, but in the hands of Jesus, nothing is too big. There is one thing that you can always give, yourself. You can be part of a miracle. You can be used for the glory of God, as you are. Be ready. Be willing. Give yourself.

> *"Commend what you do to God,*
> *And your plans will find achievement."*
>
> **PROVERBS 16:3**

TO WHOM SHALL WE GO?

"Simon Peter answered, 'Lord, who shall we go to?
You have the message of eternal life, and we believe;
we know that You are the Holy One of God.'"

JOHN 6:68-69

We live in a world that is constantly searching for answers and meaning, ignoring the truth that is plain as day. Jesus. Society is always searching for the next best thing when the greatest of all possible guarantees is right in front of us. Jesus. We look for worth and purpose in our lives when we have someone who values us for who we already are. That someone is Jesus. Peter realized where the real source of personal worth comes from, faith in the grace and mercy of Jesus.

Jesus is the only path to eternal life. We spend a lot of time chasing fads and promises from the world that never, ever can give the gift of eternal life. We put faith in powerful people that continue to disappoint us and fall short of what they promise. Peter not only recognized the message of Jesus, he believed that message as truth and directly from God. He put his faith in the One he knew would not disappoint and was worthy of his complete trust and faith. Only Jesus.

The message of eternal life from Jesus has power and promise. It is more than just acknowledging that there is God, it is following the example of Jesus and committing to Him through faith to declare Jesus as Lord and Savior for our eternity. Where do we turn when we want the truth? Jesus. Who gives us value and worth? Jesus. Who has shown mercy and grace to each of us to guarantee our eternity? Jesus.

He is God. He is eternal life. Believe and follow the Lord.

> *"Never set your foot on the path of the wicked,*
> *Do not walk the way that the evil go."*
>
> **PROVERBS 4:14**

ALL GLORY TO GOD

"To God, the only God, who saves us through Jesus Christ our Lord, be the glory, majesty, authority and power, which He had before time began, now and forever."

JUDE 25

There is nothing above or greater than God Himself. There is nothing more magnificent than God. Nothing deserves our honor, attention, praise, and obedience above God Himself. How blessed we are to be the sons and daughters of God, who loves and shows grace to each of us. His mercy, His love, and His power are always with us. We are His creation, His desire, and the focus of His grace. How amazing it is to be loved by so wonderful a creator like God.

It is very easy sometimes to forget that God is ultimately in charge of everything. God has more power than sin, more authority than anyone, and more mercy than we could ever comprehend. We spend so much time looking at our circumstances and our shortcomings that we forget that a powerful, loving God is in charge of everything. He is gracious. He is loving. He is just. He is Truth. He is above all.

He saved us through Christ and deserves our constant thanks. He created this world and each of us and deserves our constant honor. He saved us from our sins through Christ and deserves our constant praise. He loves us completely. We need to respond in faith.

God's authority, power, and majesty have always existed. He chose to not only create us, but also to love us. He is unchanging, dependable, and sovereign. He is the ultimate power. His timing is always perfect, and His promises are always secure. Life may seem like a struggle between good and evil, but we know for sure that God is already the victor and source of our eternity with Him. He is always present, knows all, and is all powerful. He is our God. He is the only thing in heaven or on earth worthy of our praise.

When you feel helpless, know that He will always be by your side. When you feel powerless, know that He is the most powerful advocate you could ever have. When you feel small, know that you are part of God's plan. When you doubt, feel reassured by His creation and rely on the work of Christ to bring you closer to Him and to a life of faith. When life feels out of control, find rest in His peace that passes all understanding. When you celebrate, give God the honor. When you accomplish, give God the praise. When you love, know that the spirit of love inside you is a gift from God. Adore Him. Praise Him. Honor Him. He is worthy of your faith.

> *"To God belong the balance and scales,*
> *All the weights in the bag are of his making."*

PROVERBS 16:11

HUMBLE YOURSELF

"Humble yourselves before the Lord and He will lift you up."

JAMES 4:10

Have you ever yearned for God to lift you up? Have you ever wondered where God was, wishing He would swoop in and come to your rescue? Can you honestly say that you have humbled yourself before the Lord?

This verse sounds so simple, yet is so contrary to our natural instincts. So much of our efforts are spent building ourselves up, desperately trying to elevate ourselves to a standard that we apply to ourselves. We want to be in charge and determine our own destiny and solutions to our problems. Our goals are our own, paying little attention to the directions that God gives us.

Does the manner in which you live characterize a life and attitude of humbleness? What do you expect God to do? God's directions are clear and His promises are reliable. Christ was the perfect example of true humility before the Lord. The sacrifice, discipline, and words of Christ give us the example of how to live our lives. It defines what it means to be humble before God. If you desire to be lifted up, then come into harmony with God and let Him reside inside you. Realize your place in God's plan. Realize that God is God. Acknowledge that we are not God.

Despite your relentless conquest to take control of your life, you will fail when you depend on yourself. As long as we put our ambitions first, we cannot be in communion with God. Our mission is to be His servant, open and ready for the direction and circumstances that God has planned for us. The realization that God is above all things and deserves our highest honor is the first step in our transition toward humbleness. God's plan is for us to serve Him in the place where He puts us, with the people around us, with the gifts He has provided.

God is ready and anxious to lift us up to complete His purposes for us if we would spend less time looking forward and more time looking up. Your humbleness before Him surrenders yourself to Him, putting you in a place where you rely on God and not yourself. It is then that your faith opens you to accept the Lord lifting you up.

God's power can never be matched by us. Acknowledge His wisdom and realize who is really in control. Let God be God, and you be His servant. He will lift you up. The fear of the Lord is the beginning of wisdom, His wisdom. Be humble and receive it.

"A man's pride brings him humiliation,
He who humbles himself will win honor."

PROVERBS 29:23

MOTIVATION

"For those who sought renown and honor and immortality by always doing good there will be eternal life."

ROMANS 2:7

What is your motivation? Do you draw attention to yourself or do your actions point others to God? Do you do what you think is right to earn your way to heaven, or do you do what is right to honor God, relying on Christ's sacrificial blood and your faith to determine your eternity? Do you get more enjoyment out of feeling good about yourself, or does your satisfaction come from knowing your actions help others? Again we should ask ourselves, what is our motivation?

Too often our motivation is based on selfishness and arrogance. Too often we do things for our own reasons, rather than following the commands of God. Too often we do things to bring praise to ourselves, rather than to God. Left to our own understanding and motivations we lose sight of the spirit that God desires for all of us.

The right action undertaken for the wrong reasons diminishes the power and efficacy of the result. Actions done with misplaced motivation become distorted and cannot reach the full potential that God intends. So often we complicate our actions with impure reasoning. We rationalize, over-think, and justify our decisions to ourselves. This removes God from the equation. Life can be so much simpler than we think if we would follow the single ideal referred to in this verse. Always do what is good! If your focus is on God, you will do good in all situations. If your focus is on yourself, you will only do good when it suits you. Eternal life is promised to those who focus on God, His promises, and His plan for salvation. Your focus will be demonstrated by your motivation. God looks past your actions and sees your reasons and determines your true desire to do good at all times.

When faced with a decision and choice we should examine our motivations and focus. We must strive to keep our reasons pure and our actions good. Let your reliance and obedience to God be your motivation and your decision to do good a witness to the glory of God. Be sure your reasons are pure, beneficial, and transparent. Keep God at your center. Always do good and be the recipient of God's promises.

> *"Let the other man praise you, but not your own mouth.*
> *A stranger, but not your lips."*
>
> **PROVERBS 27:2**

LIVING WATER

> *"Jesus replied, 'If you only knew what God is offering and who it is that is saying to you: Give me a drink, you would have been the one to ask, and He would have given you living water'."*

JOHN 4:10

It is so easy to get lost in the routine of daily life, always going to the well but never being truly refreshed. We keep plodding by day after day, not seeing Christ at the well. We have become desensitized to what our potential could be if we were to look at the source of the water, rather than the water itself. We can survive at the well, but it is Christ that gives us real life and satisfaction. It is only through Him that our thirst is quenched and we become fully refreshed.

If we changed our attitude and outlook, seeing Christ in everything, wouldn't it change everything? Instead of surviving wouldn't we be experiencing a fuller life? Instead of getting by, wouldn't we see abundance? Instead of seeing the moment, wouldn't we see eternity? Instead of a life of demands, wouldn't we see a life of opportunity? Instead of seeing the results of man, wouldn't we see the promises of His grace? With our eye on Christ, everything changes.

We never know when that moment to interact with Christ will happen. A woman doing her daily chore, fetching water came face to face with Jesus.

It is possible that we, too, may come into communion with Jesus amid a mundane task. He met her where she was. He meets us where we are as well. He is always offering living water, a love beyond belief, and a peace we cannot comprehend. He is always there. Where will you be? We live in a world that seems to be coming undone at the seams. We as believers are being challenged by the ideas of the day in a society that is doing everything it can to push God away. But He is still there…waiting…offering the living water. It is up to us to keep our hearts and minds open to Him. Seek the living water He offers. Love at every opportunity. Do not forget what Christ is offering. It is more than existence; it is a full life in Him. Let your faith open your eyes and your heart, ready to receive the living water that Christ has to offer.

> *"My son, pay attention to my words, listen carefully to the words I say; do not let them out of your sight, keep them deep in your heart. They are life to those who grasp them, health for the entire body."*
>
> PROVERBS 4:20-22

PSALM 18

Verses 1-2
Verse 30

"I love You, God, my strength,
My savior, You rescue me from violence.
God is my rock and my bastion,
My deliverer is my God."

"This God, His way is blameless;
The word of God is without dross.
He it is who is the shield
Of all who take shelter in Him."

MY FOCUS

ALLOW YOURSELF TO BE MOVED

"Everyone moved by the Spirit is a son of God."

ROMANS 8:14

What moves you? On what basis do you make your determinations? Are you open to being moved in the direction of God? What strikes a chord in your heart that spurs you into action?

A Christian possesses the Spirit of God. If you possess the Spirit of God, you are a Christian. It is that Spirit that identifies us as a son or daughter of the Almighty, a co-heir with Christ, and recipient of the full and complete grace of God. It is that Spirit that leads us forward into faith and into the new creature identified by a life in Christ. It is that Spirit that binds us to the Father and leads us away from sin. It allows us to live a life of eagerness, enthusiasm, and a willingness to love. It is His Spirit that moves us.

A life that is shut off from God and centered on self is a life that cannot separate itself from a hardened heart. Egotism and selfishness never allow for the Spirit of God to flow freely as God intended. A self-determined heart divorced from God is no more than a life of self-preservation. A life moved by God is a life of trust, love, sacrifice, and humility.

So often we try to call ourselves sons of God, yet hold on to our own worldly priorities, preconceptions, and selfishness. In this mindset, we only move for our own good and in complete defiance of God's commands and priorities. On the other hand, an open heart allows our emotions, actions, and focus to be moved and led by the Spirit. Will you let the Spirit move you?

When we let the Spirit lead us away from sin, there is freedom. When we let the Spirit move us toward Christ, there is freedom. When we let the Spirit shape our decisions and actions, we are truly sons and daughters of the Kingdom of heaven. A heart filled with the Spirit will be supple and open. It is willing to be moved in God's direction. It soaks in the goodness of God and is guided by faith. It sets its selfish desires aside, instead choosing to be obedient in love. It will be ready to be moved.

When the voice of God pulls at your heart be ready to be moved. Respond in faith. Be bold in love. Celebrate the fact that you are truly a son of God, the recipient of all the blessings associated with that grace. Be moved. Be led. Happily proclaim, "I am a child of God."

*"God created me when His purpose first unfolded,
Before the oldest of His works."*

PROVERBS 8:22

INCREASE AND IMPROVE

"My prayer is that your love for each other may increase more and more and never stop improving your knowledge and deepening your perception so that you can always recognize what is best."

PHILIPPIANS 1:9-10

Growth and maturity in our faith is something for which we should all strive. We love, but how can we emulate Jesus by loving even more? We have faith, but how can we nurture and empower our faith to be ever more on display? We trust God, but how can we deepen and depend on that trust to let His peace overwhelm us? We believe in the Word, but how can we let the power of the Word be part of our everyday motivations in all situations? God loves us with abundant, overflowing compassion. Can we do the same?

In this verse, Paul is encouraging us to understand and recognize what is best in all situations. We make many decisions, make a lot of comments, and live in a way that reflects our heart. Do we always choose what is best? Do we build up or tear down? Do we take the easy way out or do the hard work necessary for the best outcomes? Paul is praying for all of us to go beyond good…to the best. We have a God that deserves nothing but our best intentions and the best of our actions. He deserves the best of our faith and the best of our worship. He deserves the best of our attitudes and the best of our trust. He is a God that doesn't stop at goodness. He is a God that gives the best of everything.

We may all have ups and downs in our life of faith, but it is very important that we always keep growing. As we mature in our faith we can come to depend on God more and more, understand more and more, and love more and more. God never runs out of love. Neither should we. Strive for the best and let His grace, love, and mercy continue to fill you to overflowing.

"You will then understand what the fear of God is,
And discover the knowledge of God."

PROVERBS 2:5

MINISTRY

"And the king will answer, 'I tell you solemnly, in so far as you did this to one of the least of these brothers of mine, you did it to me.'"

MATTHEW 25:40

In this verse, Christ spoke directly to us about our ministry here on earth. Wouldn't our attitude be different if we realized that it was Christ Himself who was hungry, and we had the ability to feed Him? Wouldn't you feed Him? How differently would you prioritize your time if it was Christ Himself who was lonely? Wouldn't you visit Him? How concerned would we be if we knew Christ Himself was thirsty? Wouldn't we do whatever was necessary to quench His thirst?

We have these opportunities every day! The only thing limiting our ministry to Christ here on earth is ourselves. He has provided for us and it is up to us to use those gifts in ministry to Him. We as Christians should strive to meet the needs of those around us just as Christ has met all our needs. We need to keep a servant's heart, realizing that what has been given to us by God comes with a directive: it is our Christian responsibility to be good stewards of those gifts, using them to meet the needs of those we see before us.

We are not to live in isolation, hoarding our gifts and talents, finding self-satisfaction in our own worth. We are to meet the needs of others in every way. When we are focused on ministry we can easily find situations that need us to provide emotional, spiritual, and physical support. It is with an empathetic heart that we need to view the needs of others. How can we help?

Our serving attitude serves not only those in need, but it glorifies our Lord at the same time. It is for Him that we gladly humble ourselves to identify and meet the needs of others. Ours is a ministry based on obedience to Christ, purity of purpose, and love. It is to honor Christ that we deserve to be servants.

Lord, open our eyes and hearts to be ministers of Your blessings. We do it all, gladly, to glorify You.

"Do not refuse a kindness to anyone who begs it,
If it is in your power to perform it."

PROVERBS 3:27

CARRY THE TROUBLES OF OTHERS

"You should carry each other's troubles and fulfill the law of Christ."

GALATIANS 6:2

Compassion. Empathy. Selflessness. These are some of the traits of Christ that are missing from our society. The world focuses on itself. Paul is imploring us to follow Christ's example and care wholeheartedly for others. The law of Christ is to love others as we would love ourselves. That picture is hardly the vision of today's society. But we can make a difference!

Read the newspapers or watch television. It is easy to see that the focus couldn't be further from compassion. We love to hear about the troubles of others, imagining ourselves not as bad as they are. We are showered by commercials telling us we deserve the best, the newest, the fastest. They tell us that we need more and we need it now. Unspoken, but often implicit is that it all comes to the detriment of our neighbor. We are told that life is a competition. You win by beating those around you. We are told to put ourselves first and worry only about our own lives. This does not fulfill the law of Christ.

The law of Christ is love. It doesn't put the other person down to win an argument. Conversely, it is full of compassion and understanding. It looks for ways to help, even if doing so means personal sacrifice. It is displaying the love of God at every opportunity. It is honoring the sacrifice of Christ by living a life full of the principles of a believer. It is loving and forgiving, because He loves and forgives you. As a believer, we belong to Christ and enjoy the freedom to be a vehicle to pour out His love. We are overflowing in His grace with the ability to be compassionate, caring witnesses to our commitment to Him.

Caring for our neighbor is a wonderful way to fulfill Christ's law, the law of love. It should be done willingly and without grumbling. Don't be fooled into thinking that this world is all about you. We are all part of God's plan and we are empowered by the Holy Spirit. We need to care for our neighbor because Christ is in each of us. His grace, mercy, and power will shine through us as we fulfill His law, and His is a law of love. We can all make a difference in this world by being compassionate and loving to the people that God puts in front of us every day. The opportunities to show His grace are within our reach. We need to make a difference. Throw off what society expects, and do what Christ expects. Love one another.

*"The godless is forever coveting,
The virtuous man gives without ever refusing."*

PROVERBS 21:26

RENEWAL

"...and you have put on a new self which will progress towards true knowledge the more it is renewed in the image of the creator..."

COLOSSIANS 3:10

Do you ever just want to start over? Wouldn't it feel good to throw away the old stuff and bring in the new? New clothes, new furniture, a new car, or maybe better yet, an entirely new self. Wouldn't it be wonderful to take our past mistakes that we carry with us to the trash, wipe away the guilt that just never quite leaves us, and erase our disappointments that hold us back? Wouldn't a new attitude change our course and a new outlook move us in the right direction? We can make a lot of things new in our lives, but what we really need is a new self that is renewed day after day by the grace and power of God.

Permanent renewal comes from the true knowledge of God as we experience the fullness of Him and His loving grace for us. We can get new things on our own, but we can be a new person in Christ only through Him. As we gain knowledge and confidence in Him, we move forward in life, becoming a new creation and new servant of God. The quest for real peace and joy becomes tangible as we move our focus from ourselves and focus on

God. Our trust in things has failed us time and time again, but the promises of God will never falter. Our old self disappoints, but our new self satisfies. Yes, we fall back at times, but God's renewal will keep coming as we progress in our reliance on Him. We do not need new things to start over. We need Christ. We spend a lot of time looking at things through our own particular lens. We do not spend enough time looking at things through the lens of Christ. With Him we can have a new vision, a new frame of reference. With Him we can have a new freedom and a new joy. With Him we are made new creatures and enjoy all the promises of God.

Want to be renewed? Let Jesus do it. A new car gets old. New paint job fades. New clothes wear out quickly. A new self in Christ progresses and matures. True knowledge of Christ strengthens, and the power of God renews us day after day. As this world fades and disappoints, a life in Christ becomes richer and richer. Move forward in Christ with a new character and new self. He will make you new.

> *"For God Himself is giver of wisdom,*
> *From His mouth issue knowledge and discernment."*
>
> PROVERBS 2:6

TEMPTATION

"Filled with the Holy Spirit, Jesus left the Jordan and was led by the Spirit through the wilderness, being tempted there by the devil for forty days."

LUKE 4:1

Temptation: It is all around us. It is a constant reminder that the devil is real and can directly affect our lives. Thank God Jesus did not give in to His temptations! The first five words of this verse are the foundation for the results. "Filled with the Holy Spirit" tells us where the power to resist our temptations come from.

How can you possibly expect to resist the temptation unless you rely on the Holy Spirit? It takes more than personal willpower or reliance on values. These words also indicate Jesus' condition of not just being aware of the Holy Spirit, but being filled with it. There was no room for doubt or rationalization. The Holy Spirit filled Him, and left no possibility of the surrender to temptation.

Note also that the peak of the devil's efforts to tempt Jesus came when He was most vulnerable as a man. Who wouldn't want bread to eat when it had been forty days between meals? Who wouldn't want to have the glory of world kingdoms when you had been alone forty days in the wilderness?

Who wouldn't want protection from harm when faced with the dangers of the wilderness? Jesus answered confidently to all the temptations with His conviction to the words "You must not put the Lord your God to the test." There is no middle ground. You either trust God or give in to your own desires. Jesus knew who His Master was and dismissed the devil's temptations with more words. "You must worship the Lord you God, and serve Him alone."

How do we respond to temptation? You can't be partially committed and think you can choose your temptations. Do you trust God to know what is best for you or do you tend to take the easy way out? Let Jesus be your example. Rely on the one thing that stands true throughout all temptations, the Lord your God. With Him, you will persevere and claim victory over temptation.

> *"He who listens closely to the word shall find happiness,*
> *He who puts his trust in God is blessed."*
>
> **PROVERBS 16:20**

PSALM 117

"Alleluia!
Praise God, all nations,
Extol Him, all you peoples!
For His love is strong,
His faithfulness eternal."

MY FOCUS

THE EVIDENCE IS BEFORE YOU

*"Ever since God created the world His everlasting power and deity—
however invisible—have been there for the mind
to see in the things He has made."*

ROMANS 1:20

The grandeur and deity of God surround us! The evidence of God is before us! All we have to do is open our eyes and realize the scope of what God has made. Creation screams that God exists and His hand is in everything.

How blessed we are! God's creations are of such magnitude and intricacy that we have no excuse not to acknowledge the deity of God. Why do we think that there is a natural answer to every question we have? As humans, we always want to focus the answers to our questions into terms and solutions that we understand, as though that gives us control. We think that there has to be an explanation for all that is around us in terms that we can understand.

God is God! Graciously accept the wonders of His creations which can be found everywhere we look. Even though we may not directly feel God's power every day, it is nonetheless evident. To not see His power in those things around us will surely lead to misguided self-importance at the expense of belief. The more people try to explain God's creations the more empty those words become. Their rationales only move them further from the truth.

Look around and believe. Recognize that what we experience, either directly or indirectly, comes from the hand of God. Once we realize the magnitude of His power and are willing to acknowledge the enormity of God's deity, we will recognize God as supreme. This shift in attitude acknowledges God's power, not our logic, as the answer to what we need. Open your eyes and mind and know that God's presence is constant and real.

> *"Neither wisdom, nor prudence, nor advice can stand in God's presence."*
>
> PROVERBS 21:30

ALWAYS WANT PEACE

"Always be wanting peace with all people, and the holiness without which no one can ever see the Lord."

HEBREWS 12:15

Always be WANTING peace. Find a way to let peace be the ultimate goal in all our interactions. Follow it. Find it. Seek it. Let your desires be for replacing conflict and ego with harmony and humility.

Always be wanting PEACE. God does not want us in the constant state of conflict and anxiety. He desires the comfort and confidence available to all who call Christ their Lord.

Always be wanting peace with ALL people. Peace is the desirable attitude and way of life for the believer. We do not parcel out our peace to those we like or agree with. We give our peace freely and graciously, just like Christ gave completely for each of us.

Always be wanting peace with all people, AND the holiness. Peace and holiness go together, being mutually strengthened. True peace comes with the constant sanctification given to us through grace. We look to Christ for power to shield us from conflict and move us toward conformity with Him. His peace that passes all understanding comes through obedience to Him and can therefore be displayed to all people.

Always be wanting peace with all people, and the HOLINESS. Peace that comes with unholy motivation is no peace at all. As we strive to be more and more like Christ we are able to find peace in every situation. Compassion, humbleness, sacrifice, and obedience lead to peace. Knowing that our strength comes from God and He is worthy of all our praise leads to peace. Trusting and glorifying God leads to peace.

Always be wanting peace with all people, and the holiness WITHOUT WHICH no one can ever see the Lord. Believing in your heart means you have to show your faith through action. We cannot call ourselves a follower of Christ and not seek peace and holiness. An attitude of peace and the lifestyle of holiness testifies to the Lordship of Christ in our lives.

In a world that is continually in strife, we are called to be peacemakers. We are called to set ourselves apart and let Christ be the light that moves us to living a holy life. It is with a pure heart that we should find answers, avoid strife, and give glory to God. May we all find His peace.

"Bitterness is in the heart of the schemer,
Joy with those who give counsels of peace."

PROVERBS 12:20

PUT ON LOVE

"Over all these clothes, to keep them together and complete them, put on love."

COLOSSIANS 3:14

We all have talents and gifts, but they are incomplete without love. Love is the covering in our lives that gives purpose and meaning to all that we do, keeping our motives pure and our intentions genuine. When we approach our lives feeling and experiencing the love of God, we are complete. When we show our love of God by loving our fellow man, we are complete. The more we love, the more we have the ability to love more. God loves us with abundance, and it is that love that can keep all of His creation bound together in common purpose…to never stop loving.

Love is the top garment, the one that people can see because we place it on display. Love is obvious when it is put into action, and it covers many of our faults. Love is our outward declaration that we trust and depend on a loving God who expects us to love in return. Love is letting compassion and care be the first things that people see and the first things that define us as followers of Him. Love protects, shields, and strengthens us to action. It holds the body together against the challenges and difficulties we face and allows us to take on life face first, boldly, and sure of victory. A life adorned by love will be a blessed life well spent.

When we daily put on the love of God, we can be set free to love with passion and abundance, trying to mirror the essence of the love of God for each of us. His love is complete, and it binds all believers together in His grace. His love is seen through His mercy and compassion, grace and care, justice and truth. His sacrifice testifies to the depth and fullness of His love. That love is available to us! Put it on! Let it wrap around you and witness to your faith.

"Let kindliness and loyalty never leave you;
Tie them round your neck,
Write them on the tablet of your heart."

PROVERBS 3:3

THE BEST GIFT EVER

"There is no need to be afraid, little flock, for it has pleased your Father to give you the kingdom."

LUKE 12:32

What do you fear? Do you ever have enough? Are you happy with who you are, not needing to impress or conform to the ideas of others to be accepted? Do you think you need to do more and more in order to please God? This verse wipes away our misconceptions.

Every day each of us has to figure out who we trust. Do we mold God into our idea of what we need, trying to take the risk out of life to suit our comfort, or do we give ourselves over to God, knowing that no circumstance of this world can separate us from Him? Do we worry about the situations of the day and, in doing so, push God to the side, saving Him for emergencies, expecting Him to help us on demand? There is no need for our self-imposed fear. God has you covered.

The freedom that we can all enjoy comes from the actual joy of God. Our freedom does not come because we have pleased God by what we have earned. Our freedom can be realized because God finds joy in giving to each of us. It is about God, not us. Always remember the important truth that God first loved us, *while we were still sinners.* We have a God that finds joy in giving, in grace, and in His creation. His plan is love, not pride. His plan is grace, not merit. His plan is eternal, not temporary.

God has given you the Kingdom! We do not have a "just enough" God, we have a God of abundance. He is the God of "more than you can imagine" and "overflowing grace." He has spared nothing to allow each of us to be heirs with Christ, because of Christ. His timing is always perfect and His love overshadows the adversity we may experience in the here and now. We may not have everything that we might think we want, but what is important, most important, is that the supreme thing we could want is already ours. He has given you the Kingdom! It is there for the believing, ready. The perfect gift has been given. Receive it with joy. You never need to be afraid again.

> *"But whoever listens to me may live secure,*
> *He will have quiet, fearing no mischance."*
>
> **PROVERBS 1:33**

INFLUENCE

*"The life and death of each of us has its influence on others;
if we live, we live for the Lord; and if we die, we die for the Lord,
so that alive or dead we belong to the Lord."*

ROMANS 14:7

Whether we know it or not, whether we mean to or not, each of us has influence on others. A kind word, an angry response, a caring attitude all make a difference in other people's lives. Do you consider your actions and how it might affect others? We are all interconnected to many people around us, affecting attitudes and decisions every single day. What great opportunities God presents to us every day.

If you stopped to consider how your actions might affect others' lives wouldn't you be more careful about how you act? Throughout the day do you live as if you had influence over others? Do you realize the power God has granted you through your relationships?

We are blessed with the responsibility to not let our actions in any way interfere with the spiritual growth of anyone around us. We have an obligation to conduct ourselves in a manner that brings others closer to God. Don't argue about things that are unimportant or separate yourself from others because of a difference of opinion. Instead, consider what is important, and ask yourself if your influence in a given situation is beneficial or detrimental to the Lord. Be happy. Put the best construction on all situations. Your positive response in adversity gives strength to those around you. Your praise and peaceful nature can soothe the anger of others. Your neighborly love in all situations can open the hardened heart of the non-believer.

It is not our duty to pass judgment on others, but instead to open the avenues for others to mature in their faith in God. Others can see our reactions, steadfastness, conviction, faith, trust, and hope. You can be a positive influence to others, or you can be a hindrance. You belong to the Lord in everything that you do. Be sure that your influence belongs to Him as well.

> *"A good name is more desirable than great wealth,*
> *the respect of others is better than silver or gold."*

PROVERBS 22:1

GOD'S WISDOM

"If it was God's wisdom that human wisdom should not know God, it was because God wanted to save those who have faith through the foolishness of the message we preach."

1 CORINTHIANS 1:21

God wants faith from us, not wisdom. God's plan to save us is not designed to demand proof or to make intellectual sense. It is designed for faith. Nothing we can do can save ourselves, except belief in His grace. It is trust in something beyond our ability to reason and the peace that comes with that trust that is God's plan to save us.

Every time we want to understand God's plan on our own terms we diminish the power of the Gospel in our lives. We can't think our way to salvation, we accept it through faith. Will you only trust what you are capable of rationalizing and analyzing, or can you allow your heart to be changed and let the mysteries of the power of God bring you peace and salvation?

Worry comes when we dwell on our inability to predict and influence future events. Anxiety comes when we let the fear of our inadequacies dominate our actions. We repeatedly fail when we put ourselves first. There is an answer to becoming merely the result of our own shallowness. Faith.

Faith in God has the ability to change both our heart and mind. God has the ability to put things into an eternal perspective. God has the ability to bring you peace, true peace. Can you completely understand how this happens? NO! The good news is you aren't supposed to understand with your brain, you are to accept with your heart.

There will always be those that demand understanding, those who scoff at the foolishness of your faith. They do not rely on faith, and the message seems too unbelievable for them to accept. To those with faith, the message could not be more reliable. Lives change. Actions change. Attitudes change. Priorities change.

Faith is the one component of our own doing that contributes to God's plan. It is on His terms that salvation comes to us. He wants an eternal relationship with us that requires only one thing, faith. We as humans make salvation so difficult when we try to figure out everything about it. Salvation is much simpler than that. Too often it is ourselves that stands in the way of our own salvation when we don't let God be God.

Is this foolish? Perhaps to some, but not to the believer whose heart is filled with faith. God's wisdom is before each of us. Our faith will make it ours.

> *"The wicked do not know what justice means,*
> *Those who fear God understand everything."*

PROVERBS 28:5

PSALM 46

Verses 1-3

"God is our shelter, our strength,
Ever ready to help in time of trouble,
So we shall not be afraid when the earth gives way,
When mountains tumble into the depths of the sea,
And its waters roar and seethe."

MY FOCUS

COMFORT AND COMPASSION

"Blessed be the God and Father of our Lord Jesus Christ, a gentle Father, and the God of all consolation, who comforts us in all our sorrows, so that we can offer others, in their sorrows, the consolation that we have received from God ourselves."

2 CORINTHIANS 1:3-4

How do you picture God? This verse tells us of the true nature of God. He is the essence of love, care, compassion, and empathy. He knows our feelings of frustration from failure and our feelings of guilt when we fall. He is there to console us, wanting and willing to ease our minds and hearts. He is there when we are at our weakest, providing strength and perspective to support us. His gentle hand gives us the confidence to face our sorrows with the knowledge that His promises continue to be true in all circumstances. He is the God of all compassion. His love is boundless and unconditional. His comfort is always present and sincere. He is the one and only provider of true peace. Blessed be God!

So what is our response? Just as He is there to comfort us, we are to be His extension on earth by offering consolation and comfort to all those in need. When you are filled with the compassion of God, it is impossible not to feel empathy for those around you. The world is full of challenges and sorrows, but they are not debilitating to those who believe in God. Instead, these times are opportunities to display the compassion that God has bestowed on us. He is an understanding God, and He continually delivers His peace and consolation.

When you need a calming word, God's Word is there. When you need a comforting arm around your shoulder, God's presence is there to bear your burden. When it seems that all hope is gone, God's promises are there and will remain unchanged into eternity. God's consolation does not change our circumstances, but it does soothe our hearts and souls. It allows you to live with the caring character of Christ as our example, allowing us to live with and in faith.

Are you living in faith? Are you living with compassion? Are you available to offer the support that you get from the strength of Christ to those in need? The answers to these questions reveal your willingness to respond to the goodness and love of God. Be aware. Be compassionate. Be a vehicle to extend the loving arm of God to all those in need.

"Do not abandon friend, or father's friend;
When trouble comes, do not go running to your brother's house.
Better a friend near than a brother far away."

PROVERBS 27:10

THE GOD OF HOPE

"May the God of hope bring you such joy and peace in your faith that the power of the Holy Spirit will remove all bounds to hope."

ROMANS 15:13

The God of hope leaves nothing to chance. People often mischaracterize hope, especially when it comes to hope in Jesus. The hope of a Christian is more than a wish; it is an acknowledgment of the character of God. It is the understanding that God can be trusted to fulfill all His promises. It is the peace that can come from living an assured life, having already been loved by God. It is confidence in the majesty, power, and saving grace of God. I believe this, yet I struggle with my life being defined with that kind of character. Does my hope abound? Do I show real, overflowing joy? Is my mind at peace, or is my brain cluttered with all kinds of things that get in the way of living with hope?

For me, it comes down to remembering who to trust. Instead of wishing, I need to rely on Him. Instead of wishing, I need to trust in Him. Instead of wishing, I need to fully accept that my eternal future has been secured through Him. Challenges of the day come and go, but that never changes the saving grace of God. I too often fail to do the right thing, but that never changes the love of God. I know that I can have the joy and peace of God at hand, if I will only get out of the way and put Him first, not me. My struggles seem the worst when I forget that God is God, He is in control, and His mercy, love, and grace are mine for the believing. God, not me, is the author of hope. Real joy and peace are based on the character of God, not any resource of mine. Faith in Him, not me, is the only place where the peace that passes all understanding can be found.

It is up to me to open my heart to give place to the Holy Spirit. As I become more aware of His presence in my life I can find the honest meaning and responsibility of calling myself a Christian. There is power in Him, not me. With the power of the Holy Spirit there is no limit to the amount of joy I can experience. I am not confined by my abilities to find peace when I let His peace overwhelm me. I want to live with abundant, zealous, and confident joy. I want a peace so deep that the world cannot steal it from me. I want to follow the God of hope to that kind of life. Joy. Peace. The God of hope is mine.

"Hope deferred makes the heart sick,
Desire fulfilled is a tree of life."

PROVERBS 13:12

THE ONLY ONE

"For of all the names in the world given to men, this is the only one by which we can be saved."

ACTS 4:12

These were the words of Peter as he stood before the religious and cultural leaders of his day. He was talking to the important people of the day, the people that held influence and power in the local community. These were the people who thought they had the inside track to salvation and their rules and regulations were to be followed. Peter set them straight. Only Jesus.

No person in this world can save us. No individual can save themselves by what they do. This world is powerless to save. Too often we look to people with worldly power to be the answer to our problems when they have no power over your heart. We look for a new law or a new political view to change our world, when what we need is a change of heart. We look for advice from so-called authorities of this world, but forget that the real authority is God. We read books to change our minds, but forget to ask Jesus to change our spirit. We live in a world looking in the wrong places for answers, pushing God further and further away instead of pulling closer and closer to Him. It is no wonder we live in a world of turmoil. Only Jesus saves. Period.

Peter was calling out the earthly powers of that day to recognize that Jesus is above all. We may think we have power, but it cannot stand up to the saving power of His grace. No set of rules or regulations can replace a heart given to Jesus. We can live free, totally free, knowing that Jesus has already done the work of salvation for us. We can live a life covered by His grace, freely giving of ourselves for His purpose. Who has authority over you? Jesus. Who has the power to save you? Jesus. Who can provide the peace that passes all understanding? Jesus. Who will always love you? Jesus.

We live in a world that is constantly looking for truth and answers, neglecting that what really matters in life has already been answered by Jesus and it is the absolute truth. He has saved you through faith and grace. It is done. Whenever we feel self-important or superior in any way, we need to remember that Jesus is the only way to eternal life. Only He can love everyone with perfect equality and in perfect unity. He is greater than all. The saving grace of Jesus is for everyone and only He can be the way.

"Do not think of yourself as wise,
Fear God and turn your back on evil."

PROVERBS 3:7

OF COURSE

> *"A leper now came up and bowed low in front of Him.
> 'Sir', he said 'if you want to, you can cure me.' Jesus stretched out His
> hand, touched him and said, 'Of course I want to! Be cured!'
> And the leprosy was cured at once."*
>
> MATTHEW 8:2-3

Does Jesus listen to us when we are at our lowest? Of course.

Does Jesus have the power to cleanse us? Of course.

Does Jesus desire all of us to experience freedom from sin? Of course.

The first step the leper took was to realize that Jesus was worthy, powerful, and compassionate. He bowed low, willing to humble himself in his deteriorating state to ask for mercy and healing. The leper came with all his troubles in all humility, seeking the power and compassion of the ultimate source of healing. He called on Jesus, knowing that he had not earned healing, but instead needed mercy and grace. He went to Jesus.

The response of Jesus tells so much about His nature. He reached out. He touched the person most tainted and most reviled. He was immediately in close relationship with the person who felt the most pushed away by society and custom. He responded immediately and without hesitation. He saw and heard a man in despair and He showed His love. Jesus went to the leper.

It was the mercy and grace of Jesus that healed the leper. It was and is the will of Jesus to cure those who come to Him, even in an imperfect body or an imperfect heart. Our sins do not push us so far away from Jesus that He will not always show love and compassion, mercy and freedom, redemption and renewal to those who seek Him. Does He want us to experience His healing? Of course! Go to Him. Let Him touch you. Be healed.

> *"Do not think of yourself as wise, fear God and turn your back on evil: Health-giving, this, to your body, relief to your bones."*
>
> PROVERBS 3:8

EQUALLY LOVED

"And there is no distinction between Jew and Greek, slave and free, male and female, but all of you are one in Christ Jesus."

GALATIANS 3:28

All of us are under a constant curtain of scrutiny. We like to compare and contrast, rank and judge. We get grades in school and opinions on our appearance. We give our all to become a first-string athlete, an advancing administrator, or drive the newest car. We judge people by their bank account, their status, and their influence. Some we hold in high regard, while others we find expendable. We scoff at people we do not think are as religious as we are. We judge people by their gender, race, and income bracket. Where they live and what they wear become the evidence of success. How wrong we are.

Our material wealth, religious piety, and social position does not matter to Jesus. We are all the same in His eyes. We all share an equal portion of His love. He loves each with the same fullness and sincerity. He died the same death to save every single person. There are no barriers to the love of Christ. There are no prerequisites to the love of Christ. There are no special qualifications to the love of Christ. In faith, we are ALL recipients to the same Christ, the same love, the same justification, and the same atonement. His love is based on His grace, not our failures. His salvation is based on His sacrifice, not our works. He has held nothing back for us and covers all of us with His grace. Praise God that He loves a sinner like me.

We withhold love if our expectations are not met. Christ loves us in spite of our limitations. We like to think we are better than others. Christ sees the sin in all of us and loves us anyway. We think we can earn our way to heaven. Christ has already purchased your ticket. We look down on people who disagree with us. Christ provides the unity that comes from common faith in Him. In the spirit of Christ's love, let us find a way to see everyone as our equal, bound together through the grace of God.

Instead of looking for what sets us apart from others, we must try to see the same love of Christ that is shared by everyone. Look at each other as brothers and sisters of equal merit, no better and no worse, seeking and receiving the same love of Christ. His love is universal and personal. He has saved the world and has saved you. He loves us equally. We should love like He loves.

"I love those who love Me;
Those who seek Me eagerly shall find Me."

PROVERBS 8:17

SPEAK THE TRUTH

"Above all, my brothers, do not swear by heaven or by the earth, or use any oaths at all. If you mean 'yes,' you must say 'yes;' if you mean 'no,' say 'no.' Otherwise you make yourselves liable to judgment."

JAMES 5:12

The truth can, at times, seem elusive. Too many of us try to tell someone what they want to hear rather than risk offense by speaking about the way things really are. We try to cloud our commitments in shades of gray, oftentimes diluting their value. We give an answer, usually followed by an explanation or conditions that water down our commitment. We don't want to offend anyone or be ridiculed for our stance. Too many times in our society we are told not to believe what we see with our own eyes.

Where is the truth? The truth lies with God. His truth allows us to be bold and committed to our answers. Every word we utter counts with God, and we will be judged accordingly. Why do we feel it so difficult to give bold, faithful answers? By not giving direct answers we leave ourselves open to judgment. Others can twist our words to make them mean anything that they want. They can take our explanations and conditions to prove any side of an argument. Don't leave the door open for interpretation of your words. Think carefully before you answer, and then speak the truth. All of your words should be the truth. There are not two different levels of truth. Others must be able to count on your honesty in order to give full value to your words. We must be consistent with the truth so that others can depend on the reliability of our commitments.

Nothing degrades a relationship faster than not being able to trust. Words that are subject to interpretation with no level of commitment and that can change meaning can only serve to diminish the level of trust. If we are to be good stewards of the blessings that God has bestowed on us, others must be able to trust that the words we speak are the truth. Words can be used for both divisive and constructive purposes, but the truth serves God's purposes. Be sure that God can use you as an instrument to further His kingdom. Speak your words with boldness, commitment, and authority.

"A man who can control his tongue has knowledge,
a man of discernment keeps his temper cool."

PROVERBS 17:27

PSALM 51

Verses 8-10

"Instill some joy and gladness into me,
Let the bones You have crushed rejoice again.
Hide Your face from my sins,
Wipe out all my guilt.
God, create a clean heart in me,
Put into me a new and constant spirit."

MY FOCUS

SUFFERING GOD'S WAY

"To suffer in God's way means changing for the better and leaves no regrets, but to suffer as the world knows suffering brings death."

2 CORINTHIANS 7:10

Suffering means something quite different to the Christian than it does to the world. The fact that suffering can be looked at so differently is an excellent example of how faith and trust in God gives a perspective that the world cannot understand. A common definition of suffering will never be achieved by the Christian and the world.

God's Way

Suffering God's way comes from the position of humbleness and trust. Suffering is a means of growth and understanding. Although painful at the time, suffering leads us to trust God and realize how little control we really have. For those who trust God, suffering is a stage in the development of faith and hope. There are no regrets, guilt, or dwelling on a situation, but instead an inward strength is nurtured that can only come from reliance and dependence on God. How would your character be developed without being tested? The true character of a person is displayed when decisions are hard and circumstances are less than ideal. Perseverance, trust, and humility help us to understand that our hope lies in God and not in ourselves. Ego and pride play no part in suffering God's way. God has a plan for each of us and part of becoming a mature Christian may involve suffering and testing. We know that God will change us for the better when we suffer God's way!

The World's Way

The world does not think we should suffer at all. Hardships should be avoided at all costs. Only those that get in the way of our pleasure should suffer, but certainly not yourself! You deserve better! When things go wrong, the world tells you that it must be someone else's fault, there must be someone else to blame, and we should avoid taking responsibility for our own shortcomings and unthinking decisions. The world controls by guilt, and too many people feel superior when they see others suffer. With no greater purpose in sight, the world takes advantage of those who suffer and thinks that only personal pride can see you through uncomfortable situations. The emphasis is always on self.

These are two versions of suffering with two dramatically different outcomes. God's way versus the world's way. Hope versus depression. No regrets versus guilt. Eyes towards the future versus dwelling in the past.

Choose the right way to suffer. Engage in suffering God's way and you will be blessed!

> *"My son, do not scorn correction from God,*
> *Do not resent His rebuke;*
> *For God reproves the man He loves,*
> *As a father checks a well-loved son."*
>
> **PROVERBS 3:11-12**

MORE IS EXPECTED

"When a man has had a great deal given him, a great deal will be demanded of him; when a man has had a great deal given him on trust, even more will be expected of him."

LUKE 12:48

Everyone has been blessed in some way with talent or resources. Those gifts are given specially and individually by God. The biblical principle that is evident here is that we should look for ways to use our talents and resources for the benefit of others. Jesus is speaking about generosity as a virtue and tells us that with gifts comes responsibility. We are to use the gifts we have received wisely and judiciously. People in power must rule knowing the demands put upon them by the people. If one has the ability to help, they must. People with an audience need to recognize the power of their influence. Role models have to understand that their actions are magnified and held to a higher standard than others. Each of us touches the lives of others every day and we need to use our gifts positively and for the good of those around us. Much is expected.

But even more important, when someone receives a great deal in trust, they not only represent themselves, they represent the giver. This kind of gift is meant to be passed on to the benefit of those in need. Jesus trusted us with the best part of Himself, expecting us to respond in wisdom and faith. Our faith and salvation (the great deal given) should change everything about us. We no longer represent just ourselves, we are expected to represent Jesus in all that we do. Jesus gave Himself in trust to us, fully expecting our obedience, worship, and evangelism through faith. Jesus took no shortcuts and left no individual out of His sacrifice. He came to save the world, full of sinners and gave Himself in trust to us. He gave the ultimate gift. How do we represent that to the world? Much is expected.

So the question we need to ask ourselves is what expectations are we meeting? How prepared and committed to Jesus are we? Do our lives stand up in response to the "great deal" given? Jesus is the most powerful, important gift we could ever receive. We cannot let that gift go unappreciated or taken for granted. We may know our salvation, but we have to live it as well.

Most of us have received gifts beyond our imagination. We can worship freely. We have food to eat. We have a social structure that provides joy and friendship. We have so much more than we need. We have a responsibility to help meet the needs of others and pass on the love of Jesus. We should have an expectation that we will have opportunity after opportunity to be of service and be prepared to respond. When we hold, in trust, Jesus Christ in our hearts, we can do miracles. We just might be the answer to someone's prayer when we meet the expectations of Jesus.

> *"He who shuts his ear to the poor man's cry*
> *shall himself plead and not be heard."*
>
> **PROVERBS 21:13**

THE ARMOR OF CHRIST

*"Let your armor be the Lord Jesus Christ;
forget about satisfying your bodies with all their cravings."*

ROMANS 13:14

We are being bombarded every moment of every day with concerns and desires of the body. There is temptation after temptation to put the desires of ourselves above the concern for others and for God. We need protection. We need to declare to whom we belong. We need the shield of Jesus Christ.

Alone, we are subject to constant failure, and our eternity is in constant peril. Wrapped inside of Christ, we have nothing to fear and all to gain. Only Jesus has the power to protect and save us from the evils of sin that are everywhere we look. Wrapped in the love of Christ, we can live in a world of sin and still know that He promises to cover us with His righteousness and call us His own. He is our protector and security, overpowering our natural weaknesses and selfishness. His blood covers our sin. His sacrifice and victory make us the winners. We can rest in His glory and grace.

People see you differently from the world when Christ is your armor. They see it in the way you react and act, talk and listen. They see it in your humbleness and sacrifice, care and compassion. They see it in your wisdom and love. When you are wrapped in Christ you are a different creature, belonging to Him and living a life focused on Him. Are you perfect? No, of course not. But are you growing? Yes.

Even under the constant pressure we face in a society that is doing everything it can to push God away, we can stand firm in the knowledge that we belong to Him. He gives us the strength to endure hardships, ridicule, and discrimination. He gives us the ability to live a life guided by grace as the overwhelming foundation with love as its outcome. His Spirit gives us strength, dedication, and determination to live a life given to love and given to Christ. We do not belong to the world. We belong to Christ.

We are in a spiritual battle each and every day. It is our eternal destiny on the line. When we try to go to battle all by ourselves we will lose every time. With Christ as our armor, we cannot lose. When we try to solve every problem by ourselves and think we are always in control we lose sight of the power of Christ. Wrapped in Christ, our futures are secure no matter what the circumstances. We can focus on the spiritual matters of the heart. Victory is ours for the believing. Victory is ours in faith. Victory is ours in Christ. Let Him be your power and protection.

> *"He who listens closely to the word shall find happiness;*
> *He who puts his trust in God is blessed."*
>
> **PROVERBS 16:20**

STAY IN THE LIGHT

"Anyone who claims to be in the light but hates his brother is still in the darkness."

1 JOHN 2:9

Actions speak louder than words. Our priorities are made clear by the actions we take, not by what we say. We can confess our love for God all we want and still fall short. We can donate our money, our time, and our talents to the kingdom of God and still not know God.

How pure is your heart today? What unresolved conflicts reside in your soul? These conflicts have to be resolved in order to truly be in the light. Christ's light reveals everything about us. Christ's light demands purity. If we are a true believer we have to believe the whole truth, not just the parts that fit our needs and circumstances. How much damage has been done to the kingdom of God through Christian hypocritical behavior? It diminishes not only new potential Christians who judge you by your behavior, but also fellow Christians. We must have pure, humble hearts. Our determination to hold grudges or judge others only serves to keep us further from knowing God.

Examine your heart today. Find the things that keep you in darkness. After you find them, do something about it. First, pray about them, and then humble yourself to action. Forgive if you need to forgive, ask for forgiveness if you need to be forgiven. Find a way out of your darkness into God's glorious light. May we go through the day keeping a pure heart.

*"To God belong the balance and scales,
all the weights in the bag are of His making."*

PROVERBS 16:11

KNOW WHO YOU ARE

*"...What we are is plain to God,
and I hope it is also plain to your conscience."*

2 CORINTHIANS 5:11

You cannot fool God. Sometimes we can fool ourselves, talking ourselves into rationalizing our behavior. But God cannot be fooled. We cannot rationalize our behavior before God and expect to sneak sin by Him. He knows your heart, not just your actions. God does not have a hard time figuring you out. You are plain to God with no mysteries.

Are you plain to yourself? We need to be aware of our conscience and sharpen our ability to alter our behavior. Do you know the pureness of your heart and your intentions? The moment you hesitate and wonder if something is wrong you must stop. We cannot rationalize our actions and somehow turn a sinful behavior into something pleasing in the eyes of the Lord. There are no shades of gray in your heart. The doubt tells us it is wrong. Do not give yourself the chance to deceive yourself into a wrong behavior.

Be plain to yourself. God is not fooled and neither should you be. Too many times we think that we can reveal whatever parts of our being that we want to. But God sees us deeper than we see ourselves. He knows our motives, our strengths, and our weaknesses. Let us strive to be plain to ourselves.

Acknowledge your motives and listen to your conscience. Do not fool yourself today. Be as plain to yourself as you are to God. When we know that God sees us for who we really are, let yourself be open to His mercy. May our openness before God renew our hearts to dedication to His will. Remember, you cannot fool God!

*"The plans of virtuous men are honest,
the intrigues of the wicked are nothing if not deceit."*

PROVERBS 12:6

SLOW TO ANGER

*"My dear brothers, take note of this:
Everyone should be quick to listen, slow to speak and slow
to become angry, for man's anger does not bring about
the righteous life that God desires."*

JAMES 1:19-20

How many times have we wished we could take back words spoken in anger? How many times have we been talking when we should have been listening? Anger immediately changes our perceptions and understanding. Angry people do not foster spirits of tolerance and cooperation.

Be quick to listen. How can we be empathetic or have any kind of understanding when we don't listen? Notice listening is the first priority, something necessary for us to be slow to anger. Listening is necessary for us to have a complete perspective.

Be slow to speak. What a powerful tool our tongue is. It can bless and give comfort, or it can tear down and cut like a knife. Once words are spoken, the effects are irreversible. That is why we must be sure of what we want to say! Quick words spoken in anger can be so divisive. Angry words have no mercy, no perspective, and can only do harm. Patient words, thoughtful words, and understanding words further the kingdom of God.

Be slow to anger. Self-control of our emotions gives us time for understanding. Nothing good comes from anger. Reactions are magnified and decisions are distorted. Give yourself the chance to make a good decision and be slow to anger.

Make every attempt today to be a listener. Do more than wait patiently to talk. Engage in active listening. Then choose your words with care, using them only in the most positive way. Keep control of your emotions and keep anger from your heart. Your self-control will be a blessing.

*"A mild answer turns away wrath,
sharp words stir up anger."*

PROVERBS 15:1

PSALM 8

Verse 1
Verses 3-6

"God, our Lord,
How great Your name throughout the earth!"

"I look up at Your heavens, made by Your fingers,
At the moon and stars You set in place-
Ah, what is man that You should spare a thought for him,
The son of man that You should care for him?
Yet You have made him little less than a god,
You have crowned him with glory and splendor,
Made him lord over the work of Your hands,
Set all things under his feet."

MY FOCUS

SPIRITUAL THINGS

*"Therefore we teach, not in the way in which philosophy is taught,
but in the way that the Spirit teaches us:
we teach spiritual things spiritually."*

1 CORINTHIANS 2:13

There is not a philosophy or theory that can save you. You cannot reason your way to salvation. The gift of salvation is spiritual in nature and the lessons taught by the Word are spiritual. The lessons of the world are applicable only to worldly things.

Time and time again we are told in the Word that you are to concentrate on spiritual lessons which have eternal significance. The things of the world are fleeting, but spiritual matters are forever. Do you look for chances to learn spiritual things? How high on your priority list are the lessons of the Spirit? Are you willing to be taught in faith?

Do not rely on reason, logic, philosophy, or any earthly authorities. Your salvation is assured because of grace, a fact that can only be accepted by faith. To the unbelievers who rely on their own wisdom, salvation cannot be explained. But to the believer, who relies on Spirit, salvation is a gift accepted by faith.

How much do you rely on your own wisdom? Are you willing to accept the lessons of the Spirit? You must understand that there is a higher power than yourself, and let God be God. Open yourself to learning the spiritual lesson, spiritually.

> *"He who despises the Word will destroy himself,*
> *he who respects the commandment will be safe."*
>
> PROVERBS 13:13

HIS GRACE IS ENOUGH

"My grace is enough for you: My power is at its best in weakness."

2 CORINTHIANS 12:9

No one likes to admit to their weaknesses. No one likes to admit they are not in control. Most of us think we have more power than we actually have.

Paul, in his letter to the Corinthians, had a different idea. He welcomed his weakness as a means of acknowledging that all the power we need is available through God. His weakness made him more aware that God's grace and power could be his because of his dependence on God instead of himself. Paul knew that our weakness can be covered by the power of God.

This verse is one of great comfort. God assures us that His grace and power will support, protect, and cover us in our weakest moments. When our body is broken, His power can heal and comfort us. When we are emotionally depressed, His Holy Spirit can lift us up. When we are spiritually weak, He can fill us with His power that surpasses our understanding. Our power and strength have limitations, but God's grace and power are limitless. It is at our weakest times that we realize that we have to rely on God's power instead of our own efforts.

It is at our weakest times that we have to acknowledge God as the source of what is right and true. It is at our weakest time that we must humble ourselves and admit that we can't do it all alone. What God has to offer us is all that we need. His power, His grace, and His promises are enough. There is no shame in being weak when we let God's power and grace cover us. Without acknowledging our weakness we cannot come to true dependence on God. We need God's grace! We need God's power! We need the humbleness necessary to admit it!

Insisting on our own limited power can only lead to failure. Reliance on His power will lead to peace. Thinking you can save yourself leads to pride and self-importance. Accepting God's grace leads to humility and obedience. His power is the path to contentment and peace. It is in our weakness that we have to admit the truth. God's grace is enough and His power is beyond our understanding.

> *"He who listens closely to the Word shall find happiness,*
> *He who puts his trust in God is blessed."*
>
> **PROVERBS 16:20**

LET GOD BE GOD

"How rich are the depths of God—how deep His wisdom and knowledge—and how impossible to penetrate His motives or understand His methods!"

ROMANS 11:33

Why do we find it so hard to accept the fact that God is God? He is more powerful, more understanding, more patient, and more forgiving than any of us could ever hope to be. His capabilities go far beyond our understanding and even our ability to understand. God's abilities and essence can be described in a single word: more.

Time after time we try to keep God at our level, expecting all that He does and all that He has done to make sense to us. Shouldn't God be logical? Shouldn't God always make sense to us? Shouldn't God's plan be what I have in mind? Think again.

How arrogant we are! Our narrow perspectives and expectations can limit our knowledge and understanding of God. Let God be God! He does not have the same limited perspective that we have. He does not have to impress us nor explain Himself to us. We cannot fully understand what is beyond our ability to comprehend.

What you should know is that God has revealed Himself to us in such a manner as to give us everything we need to be saved. He has given us, through His Son Jesus Christ, salvation and redemption. It is not our job to fully understand God, but instead to believe. Open yourself to the possibilities that God presents and let Him use you as part of His method as He desires. Trust His divine wisdom to be in your best interest. Allow God's greater knowledge to be inspirational in every circumstance. We have plenty of information in the Word as to how we are to behave. God has given us the example of Jesus Christ to show us the perfect life. Believe that we are the sons and daughters of the Almighty God and trust Him.

God is more. Accept, believe, and trust in Him. Let God be God.

> *"Fear of God gives good ground for confidence,*
> *in Him, His children find a refuge."*
>
> PROVERBS 14:26

EYES OF YOUR MIND

> *"May He enlighten the eyes of your mind, so that you can see what hope His call holds for you, what rich glories He has promised the saints will inherit."*
>
> EPHESIANS 1:18

Why is it so hard to prioritize the things that matter most? Why are we so easily distracted, spending our time and energy on things that in the long run really do not matter that much? We get caught up in the details of life, often missing the big picture and not appreciating the larger blessing we have in Christ. Where is your heart? It is all about the power and love of God. Jesus sets us straight. "Set your hearts on His kingdom first." We were not created to worry, but instead to experience His goodness. We were not created to see the problems of the day, but instead to long for and live for the eternal life with Christ that awaits us. We were not created to be in conflict, but instead to have the peace and love of Christ dwelling inside of us, no matter what the circumstances. It is all about priority.

If we try to find our own righteousness, we will always be frustrated in our failure. The righteousness of God is a gift which extends to every believer through faith. It is a gift, resonating inside us, guiding us through our struggles, reminding us that Christ has already won all the battles. He is our righteousness. As we trust in His righteousness we can have a different perspective of life and its troubles as we find His love and His peace dwelling in our hearts. It is all about trust and obedience.

So many things get in the way of our faith in God if we do not let Him rule us at our innermost being. As we look at everything through the lens of Christ and what He has done for us, we can find the peace that passes all understanding. See things through the eyes of what God intends for you, and set your heart in obedience to Him. Live free in the righteousness your faith in Him provides, and push the distractions aside that get in your way of trusting Him. Trust Him to provide what you need, when you need it, and how you need it. The heart set on the Kingdom and His righteousness will never fail. It is all about trust.

> *"More than all else, keep watch over your heart,*
> *Since here are the wellsprings of life."*

PROVERBS 4:23

HE IS WAITING

"Ask, and it will be given to you; search, and you will find; knock, and the door will be opened to you."

MATTHEW 7:7

It is all there waiting for us. He is there waiting for us. He is waiting for us to participate. He is waiting for us to engage with Him. He is waiting for us to take action.

We expect God to intervene on our behalf to keep us from hardship and pain, meet our daily needs, and give us peace. The problem is, we expect Him to act without us being part of the process. God wants relationship with us. He wants to communicate with us daily. He craves a closeness with us that goes beyond our wants and desires. He wants us to desire, trust and depend on Him. He wants us to know that He is the source of our peace and joy. He is waiting. Where are you?

He is there, wanting to wash us clean, waiting for our commitment and trust. He is there, able to give us peace and joy, waiting for us to accept. He is there, with all His love, waiting for us to respond. And there He is, despite our slowness or unwillingness to commit, always there, patiently present. Where are you?

The verse says to ask! A commitment to prayer keeps our communication alive with God. It is time set aside for honest, open dialog. It is that personal, intimate time that builds relationships and dependence. His promise is to meet your needs, as a loving Father would do, and to do so abundantly.

After asking, we search! His promise is clear. When we feel alone, He will not abandon us. He is there for the finding, if we are willing to look. We should strive for growth in our relationship with Him, always searching for a depth of communion with Him.

Finally, we should knock! It takes commitment to knock. It is saying "God I am here. I want to be with you." It is making yourself known as someone who desires contact and closeness. It is presenting yourself as you are and asking to come inside.

This verse gives such comfort and confidence to anyone willing to act. He is there, waiting. What are you waiting for? He promises to meet our needs, to never abandon us, and to enter into a relationship with us. He offers us eternity. Take the step of commitment and receive, find, and feel the relationship with God that awaits. He is waiting. What will you do?

"Every word of God is unalloyed,
He is the shield of those who take refuge in Him."

PROVERBS 30:5

SLAVES OF GOD

"Now, however, you have been set free from sin, you have been made slaves of God, and you get a reward leading to your sanctification and ending in eternal life."

ROMANS 6:22

There is always a driving force in our lives that influences our decisions and actions. That force becomes part of our character as we routinely give in and act according to that force. Christ came to overcome and have victory over the sin in this world that tries to control us. And He won! Now the question is whether we will replace that sinful force within us with the victorious power of Christ. You can call it slavery or influence or whatever, but something drives all of us. Let that drive be one that comes from God.

The prize of God's victory is sanctification. His victory sets us apart to be used by Him for His purposes in His kingdom. Daily we strive to become more and more like Christ, striving to mirror His character at every opportunity. He did the work. We receive the prize. Through our dedication to Him we become tied to holy causes, bearing the fruits of the Spirit as testimony to His greatness.

We once belonged to sin, but we can now belong to God. Sin leads to death. God is life eternal. Obedience to sin is restraining, while obedience to God is pure freedom. Because of Christ, we are free to live in love, giving of ourselves freely and happily. We have our reward, guaranteed through the blood of Christ. Because of Christ we can rid ourselves of guilt and shame, knowing we are new creatures fully forgiven. Because of Christ we can receive freedom from the worry, anxiety, and depression that were tied to sin.

We are truly set apart, sanctified, renewed creatures when we give ourselves to Christ. Obedience turns from obligation to joy when Christ is the object of our worship and thanks. We are alive in Christ, putting the chains of the death that comes from sin behind us. The greatest prize of all, eternal life with God, has already been secured for us and it is ours through faith.

With so many thoughts and ideas trying to get our attention, we must focus on the one thing that is most important. Christ. He is the influence, the object of our full attention, and the reason for how we approach life. A slave to God? Absolutely. We have already received the reward. Now it is time to live like the prize is ours.

> *"No man is made secure by wickedness,*
> *But nothing shakes the roots of virtuous men."*
>
> **PROVERBS 12:3**

PSALM 130

Verses 3-6

"If You never overlooked our sins, God,
Lord, could anyone survive?
But You do forgive us:
And for that we revere You.
I wait for God,
My soul waits for Him,
I rely on His promise,
My soul relies on the Lord
More than a watchman on the coming of dawn."

MY FOCUS

ETERNAL THINKING

"If our hope in Christ has been for this life only, we are the most unfortunate of all people."

1 CORINTHIANS 15:19

If we do not believe in eternity, there is no need for Christ. If we do not feel the need for forgiveness, there is no need for Christ. If we put our faith only in ourselves, there is no need for Christ. Without an eternal perspective, there is no need to sacrifice, show compassion, or love. We were created with a special ability; to know and feel the presence of God. We can filter our ambitions and intentions in this world through a lens that has eternal aspirations and expectations. We do what we do and believe in who we believe in because eternal life is not a concept or idea, it is real. We aspire to a relationship with God that never ends and never fails. How unfortunate life would be without faith in anything beyond ourselves.

What is life without faith? Without Christ, where is forgiveness? Without Christ, where is the hope? Without Christ, where is peace? Without Christ, where is joy? Without Christ, there is no need for eternal thinking.

Eternity is not something in the future, we are already in the midst of it. We already possess a spiritual soul that always continues. Our future spent with God has been promised, assured, and made real through Christ. Faith in Christ is not for the moment, it is for eternity. Faith in Christ sees us through the day and into eternity. The power of Christ sustains us today and assures our eternity. Our hope is in Christ, true God of today and of eternity. In Him, we can find peace and rest, today and for all eternity.

If we believe that Christ was only for this life, we miss the entire point of His work. His sacrifice was for our eternity. He took the sinner of today and made him able to experience the love of Christ forever. His sacrifice was our eternal righteousness. His gift was our reconciliation forever. His saving grace was our pathway to eternal life with Him. He saves today. He always saves. He saves forever.

We all have troubles and tribulations as we go through life, and it can be discouraging if we have a view that this life is all there is. Christ promises there is more. Rest in that assurance, hold on to His grace, and know that our future is one that goes on forever, held in the arms of Christ and His love.

"Do not let your heart be envious of sinners
but be steady every day in the fear of God;
for there is a morrow, and your hope will not be nullified."

PROVERBS 23:13-14

STAY AWAKE

"And what I say to you I say to all: Stay awake!"

MARK 13:37

Be ready. Be prepared. Be on guard. Be engaged. Stay awake!

None of us know the future. No matter how smart we think we are, there is nothing guaranteed in this worldly life. Our tendency is to push aside anything that we do not see right in front of us. The problems and challenges of our lives too often exclude the big picture. We focus on the present and past, while forgetting what Christ has done for all of eternity. Are you ready?

Crises reveal the real truth that we are not prepared. We think we have everything under control, only to be caught off guard by something we had never even considered. Being prepared for Christ means that we daily depend on Him for comfort. It means that we daily model our lives to be in the most harmony with Christ. It means we daily seek out ways to "do good" in every situation put before us. It means daily surrendering to a life in Christ as opposed to focusing on self. It means knowing the value of a relationship with Him. Are you prepared?

Bad things will happen. Sin is an ever-present reality. The world pushes us further and further from God at a time when we need Him the most.

Do not let those influences destroy your relationship with Christ. Every day is a day to be on heightened alert for your faith. Be aware of the potential detriment to your soul when you do not stay awake and on guard. Look at all outside influences through the lens of faith and stewardship instead of selfishness. Do not let instant gratification replace a readiness to accept the path that leads to eternity with Christ. Be on guard.

Staying awake requires action and includes finding wisdom during difficulties and faith at all times. Embrace the life that God has for you, and find His love that surrounds you. Mere knowledge and intellect can never replace compassion and love. We are called to stay awake in order to serve. We are called to action and called to wisdom. How engaged are you?

Staying awake for Christ is putting your full hope in Christ. It is a faithful reliance on a loving God. It is finding God in every situation and letting God be God. It is realizing the salvation that comes through faith in Christ and living that faith with our entire being. Staying awake for Christ is our response to God. Keep your eyes focused on Him and prepare yourself for the peace and joy that can be yours now and forever. Stay Awake!

"By kindliness and loyalty atonement is made for sin;
With the fear of God goes avoidance of evil."

PROVERBS 16:6

DO YOU BELIEVE THIS?

"I am the resurrection. If anyone believes in me, even though he dies he will live, and whoever lives and believes in me will never die. Do you believe this?"

JOHN 11:25-26

Do you truly believe this? A question that has been pondered by men over the centuries is answered in these two verses. Man yearns for eternal life. Is the answer really this simple? We must just believe? Of course it is that simple. The real question is does the manner in which you lead your life demonstrate your belief? What does it really mean to believe in Christ? Do you both believe and live in Him? If so, can anybody tell?

Christ has done everything necessary for our salvation, and the gracious gift of eternal life is ours for the believing. But the evidence of real belief and commitment reveals itself in our actions, attitudes, and humbleness.

We like to think we are important and have a sense of pride. We admire fame and fortune, sometimes sacrificing relationships for the sake of material things. We long for the newest fashions, means of transportation, and vacation destinations. We let money be a driving force in our lives. Christ asks you to be humble, forgiving, and content. Do you believe this?

Today's society influences us to put ourselves first, telling us that life is about you and your happiness. Society tells us that politics and government must separate themselves from belief in God. We are being programmed to want more and more, often at the expense of others. Christ came as a servant. God humbled Himself in the flesh for sinners, willing to sacrifice all for our benefit. Do you believe this?

Verdicts and lawsuits are often settled by twisting the truth to the point where there is no real right or wrong. We tend to rationalize our behavior: "I didn't hurt anyone," or "I won't get caught," or "everyone else is doing it." Morality has become more and more subjective and ethical behavior has been eroded to a position of weakness. Christ spoke nothing but truth. He placed honesty, morality, and relationships ahead of personal gain. Do you believe this?

If we really believe in Christ and really are living in Christ, the evidence will be unmistakable. Let your life reflect the love of Christ through you to all those around you. Put complete trust in Him, not in your own ambitions or the world around us. Your actions and attitudes will declare your belief that Christ is truly the resurrection, and you have accepted His gift of eternal life with true belief. You will live forever in and through Him. Do you believe this?

"A man's conduct may strike him as pure,
God, however, weighs the motives."

PROVERBS 16:2

CLOSE AT HAND

"The time is fulfilled, and the kingdom of God is close at hand. Repent, and believe the gospel."

MARK 1:15

This verse speaks on a couple of levels. First, it communicates a fulfillment of prophecy and a declaration of a time in history. Second, it addresses each of us today with just as much impact. The time is fulfilled. Jesus was the culmination of the promises from before and was marking His authority and importance. Today these words remind us that there is no reason to look for future events or put off our commitment to Him. The time for our response to Him is NOW. He has done everything necessary, no promise has been unmet, and no obstacles to our salvation remain. The time is NOW.

Jesus declares that the kingdom of God is not some far-off ideal, or state of mind. Jesus Himself is within reach, personally and intimately available to every believer. He resides closely, within reach, never too far away. He is within our reach and ready to provide, protect, and comfort. He is near, strengthening, guiding, and encouraging. Too often we spend time thinking of Christ as being in some far-off distant place, but this is not the case. He is with each of us, close at hand, available at all times. Wherever we are, He is there also.

The last part of this verse simplifies what we try to make so hard. It puts in five words a synopsis of what our life in Christ is all about. Too often we put up our own barriers and our own ideas about salvation. We like to compare ourselves to others, make excuses, and rationalize behaviors. The words of Jesus however tell us what real truth is and the way to approach our life. We must repent and believe the Gospel.

If we would repeat just two words from this verse throughout the day, we could keep the perspective that God is close at hand. Repent. Believe. Christ has done everything else for you already.

"Let faithful love and constancy never leave you:
Tie them round your neck, write them on the tablet of your heart."

PROVERBS 3:3

WHO DO YOU SAY I AM?

"'But you', He asked, 'who do you say I am?'
Peter spoke up and said to Him, 'You are the Christ.'"

MARK 8:29

This is the basic question that is the root of our entire being. Who is Christ to you? The way you answer will determine your actions, motivations, and priorities in life. It will set the foundation for your faith, convictions, and reasoning. It will reveal your eternity.

Is He your truth, the one that shines brightly through your commitments? Is He at the center of all that you do? Is He more than just words, but a way of life? Is He above all things to you? For whom are you living?

This passage strikes at the heart and soul of every person. It is all about faith. Your answer will determine how you handle adversity and how you can live in joy and hope in any situation. This passage makes it personal and intimate. No other person or thing can determine your own personal relationship with Him. It makes you commit and provides the principles on how you will live your life. Is this life all about you, or is it all about Him?

Too often we profess with our mouths but do not commit with our actions. It seems much easier to put ourselves first and relegate Christ to a safety net, calling upon Him only when we are in need. There is no fooling

Him because our actions and attitudes shout out loudly who we really think He is.

If He is the true God, do we give Him the reverence and honor He deserves in every situation? If He is our true Savior, do we live our lives as saved beings, happily sacrificing for the benefit of others? If He is our comforter, do we always look to Him first for the assurance of His promises? If He is our redeemer, do we thank Him continually and make every effort to live in the light of His grace?

How passionately do you display your relationship with Him? Are you like Peter, the first to speak up and declare "You are the Christ," or have you become satisfied with a comfortable level of commitment that avoids taking a bold stand for Him? Is yours a life that can be characterized as fully committed, acknowledging that He is truly the Christ, your Savior? Peter was ready for service and committed to his Lord. There was no hesitation in his testimony. Is there any hesitation in yours?

So many questions that need to be answered demand our attention. Take the time to consider who you say He is, and how your life is influenced by your declaration. This passage brings everything into a simple commitment. Your answer is yours alone and sets the foundation for your entire life and your eternity. Who do you say He is?

"He who listens closely to the word shall find happiness;
He who puts his trust in God is blessed."

PROVERBS 16:20

REMAIN FREE

"When Christ freed us, He meant us to remain free."

GALATIANS 5:1

Christ freed us once and for eternity with His sacrificial gift to us. No longer do we need to be slaves to the temptations of this world, sin, or our weaknesses. His strength and sacrifice is sufficient!

What is standing in the way of your freedom? Why do we allow our lack of trust in Him to cause anxiousness and uncertainty in our lives? What is Christian freedom? It is the freedom to love, unconditionally, without desire for payback. It is the freedom to serve, being humble enough to be used for His purposes. It is the peace that can only come from putting your entire trust in Him, rather than yourself. Christian freedom gives us so many opportunities to be His witness in this world. It takes away the restrictions that we place on ourselves and gives meaning to life. It gives us a quality that leads to displaying the character of Christ. Christian freedom acknowledges that God is in control and that all things will be used for His greater good when we follow Him. Freedom lets us experience firsthand the power of the love of God.

So many things that surround us make us slaves. Our culture, with its ever-changing morals and standards, enslaves us when we conform to its expectations. Our desire for the material things of this world enslaves us to a life of selfishness. Our lack of trust in God enslaves us to a life where we only depend on ourselves, discounting and dismissing the fact that God plays an active role in our lives and has a plan for each of us. What has you in bondage? Is it money? It is your job? Are you consumed by your own image? Does the culture make you conform to its image? Examine your motivations. Do you approach the day feeling free to do God's work, blessed with another day of opportunities, or is your approach one of obligation, doing what you feel compelled to do for your own satisfaction? We were meant to be free, and we can be! We can be free to serve and free to live as God's child, with possibilities beyond our imagination. What a blessing! Hold on to that freedom that Christ has provided and cherish it. Live freely!

*"A man's heart plans out his way
But it is God who makes his steps secure."*

PROVERBS 16:9

PSALM 56

Verses 3-4

Verses 10-11

"Raise me up when I am most afraid,
I put my trust in You;
In God, whose word I praise,
In God I put my trust, fearing nothing;
What can men do to me?"

"This I know: that God is on my side,
In God, whose word I praise,
In Yahweh, whose word I praise,
In God I put my trust, fearing nothing;
What can man do to me?"

MY FOCUS

REALLY DIED WITH CHRIST?

"If you have really died with Christ to the principles of this world, why do you still let rules dictate to you, as though you were still living in the world?"

COLOSSIANS 2:20

What is important? What separates Christians from non-Christians? Do we allow human doctrines and regulations to get in the way of our salvation? If we have really died with Christ, why do we continue to place unwarranted importance on differences in human opinions?

Anytime we set ourselves apart from others because of human doctrines, we do a disservice to Christianity. Anything that gets in the way of the Good News of salvation is to be avoided. It doesn't matter if it is human rules and regulations, superstitions or tradition. The sacrifice of Christ has set us free from man-made rules. Do not let your own self-imposed rules be a roadblock to bringing others to Christ. We are all part of the same body, and using your efforts to set yourself apart and condemn others for not following your traditions will only lead to division and divisiveness. As different people worship in different ways, we only need to ask ourselves if our actions are focused on glorifying God. Do not demand others conform to your own ideas of worship, thereby thinking yourself better than anyone else.

Christ has done the work. He has made the rules and regulations of men irrelevant. Let your desire to be in the company of all Christians and the common bond of the grace of God bind all together. Traditions are important, but not important enough to separate you from other Christians or be a hindrance to the nurturing and maturing of others. We are all partners in Christ's death and resurrection. Look for ways to build up others. Share in the victories of Christ.

*"For the man who finds me finds life,
he will win favor from God."*

PROVERBS 8:35

COUNTING ON US

"Well then, brother, I am counting on you, in the Lord; put new heart into me, in Christ."

PHILEMON 20

When you are running on empty, where can you look for refreshment? You should look to the restorative power of the love of Christ. When you see someone down or in need, how can you refresh them? The power of the love of Christ is beckoning. We do not need to look at a program or institution to act on our behalf, the answer lies through Christ IN US. Christ does not depend on a religion, He depends on US. Christ does not depend on luck, He depends on US. We have the power to use the love of Christ to refresh, renew, and strengthen those around us. Through Christ we have the power to bring hope, joy, and truth to those in need. Christ is counting on us to do His will and fulfill His plan. Are you ready to step up?

Too often we look to blame others, blame circumstances, or blame God when our heart is in need. Too often we do not demonstrate the love of Christ in the way we act, think, or talk. Too often we lose sight of the joy, peace, and rest that can be found only in Him. Our actions towards others with a loving heart can renew their spirit and let the power of Christ shine through us. Faith is not passive. Faith is a work in progress. Faith is a way of life, a way of thinking, and a way of depending on Christ. Christ is counting on us to be a refreshment to everyone we touch and an example of the power of His love. Stop looking around for someone else to step up. He is counting on you.

When we witness an act of love we are refreshed. When we see acts of selflessness we are comforted. When we see acts of sacrifice our hearts are touched. When we perform for Christ in obedience, we find rest in Him. Each of us has the ability to act in love, actively refreshing and comforting those around us. Talk is great, knowledge is great, but loving action is the true proof of our commitment to God. It is time to act.

Maybe today is the day that your action will touch the heart of someone around you. Your kindness may change a mind. Your sacrifice may soften a soul. Your commitment to Christ may help open a pathway for someone to faith. As insignificant as we sometimes feel, we must remember that Christ is in us and His power is real, overwhelming, and strong. In this verse, Paul was letting Philemon know that Philemon's acts of kindness would change hearts and refreshing spirits. Acts of love and kindness have their own power, based on the love of Christ, which can do more than we ever imagine. Actively love.

Be free with your faith and free with your love. Jesus is counting on you. Accept the challenge and let the love of Christ always chart your ways. Refresh.

> *"A kindly glance gives joy to the heart,*
> *Good news lends strength to the bones."*
>
> **PROVERBS 15:30**

PERSEVERE

*"Be persevering in your prayers and be thankful
as you stay awake to pray."*

COLOSSIANS 4:2

Prayer life is relentless. It does not depend upon outside influences or situations, but instead focuses on the relationship and hope in God. Prayer cuts through the bad news of the day and the unhappy circumstances that we may find ourselves in. Prayer is conversation and openness. Prayer is dependable and honest. Prayer opens our spirit.

When everything around us seems to be out of control, we should pray. When we celebrate because things in our lives could not be better, we should pray. When we see injustice and hardship, we should pray. When we feel far away from God, we should pray. When we feel closer than ever to God, we should pray. When we suffer, we should pray. In our most joyous moments of celebration, we should pray. At all times and in everything, we should pray.

A relentless prayer life is a good indication that we recognize that all things come from God. He is the focus of our lives and we find our complete hope in Him. So often we think of prayer as a want list of things we expect or demand God do for us. We often ask ourselves why we bother to pray. We get caught up in the demands of day-to-day life and forget that God even exists.

We forget to pray. We forget to be thankful for all we have and focus on what we think we want. We too often do not trust God. At times like these, it is time to go back to the foundation of our souls. It is a time to persevere in our weakness and know that God will provide. It is time to stay awake and be focused on what is really important, our relationship to Him. It is time to pray.

A thankful heart changes us from the inside out. It lightens our load, recognizing that we really are blessed people, because despite anything else, God loves us. A relentless commitment to thanking God has the power to change our outlooks and attitude and is infectious. A thankful heart is willing to sacrifice for others. A thankful heart is willing to love when not expected. A thankful heart is willing to put selfishness aside and find contentment with what we have. A thankful heart testifies to the character, majesty, and power of our God. Pray expectantly and thankfully.

Prayer needs to be a priority and a routine part of our lives. Communicate to God how you are feeling, your needs, your concerns, and your joys. Thank Him for the eternal life He has given, the gift of life here on earth, and His love. Call upon Him in times of need and sadness, but also during the seasons of fulfillment and joy. Prayer is about relationship and intimacy. Be relentless. Be committed. Be thankful. God is worth your time.

*"God stands far from the wicked,
But He listens to the prayers of the virtuous."*

PROVERBS 15:29

DO WHAT IT SAYS!

*"Do not merely listen to the Word, and so deceive yourselves.
Do what it says."*

JAMES 1:22

The Word is more than mere words on a page; it is alive. It is full of action. The Word takes on life when we do what it says. Simply reading or listening to the Word does little to change your life and even has less effect on the lives of others. But putting the Word into action begins a wonderful chain of change, both for you and for others. Your actions in the Word lets the Word become part of your being. Your actions become known by others, thereby letting Christ be revealed through you. Your actions in the Word can change lives, enabling others to come to faith through Christ.

If you think you can think yourself into receiving salvation you are deceiving yourself. We are saved by grace, through Jesus Christ. We must commit ourselves to live in Christ, living and doing as the Word reveals. We are not told to think godly thoughts, we are told to live in Christ. This requires action! Your actions tell you what is really important to you. What you put into practice reveals much about your priorities.

We are given a direct command, "Do what it says." We are called to action, action in the Word. Will your actions today reveal the depth of your commitment to others? Will your actions further the kingdom of God? Before you act, think of the power that your actions have. First, you must listen, but then you have to act. May your actions today serve the will of God and reveal God in all His glory.

> *"Commend what you do to God,
> and your plans will find achievement."*
>
> PROVERBS 16:3

DON'T GET STUPID

> *"The more they called themselves philosophers, the more stupid they grew, until they exchanged the glory of the immortal God for a worthless imitation, for the image of moral man, of birds, or quadrupeds and reptiles."*
>
> ROMANS 1:22

Science is exploding in the 21st century. Exciting discoveries are made every day. The flip side of this coin is that scientific theories are also reported as verified truth. They dominate media headlines and stir national debate. Out of all of this, one thing is absolutely clear. The more we know, the more evidence there is about how much we don't know.

God is beyond our understanding and until we accept this truth, we will continue to wallow in our own ignorance. Time after time, man's theories are dashed by the realization of the complexity of this world. As man searches for the origins of life, he continues to miss the meaning of life and the evidence of God's creative power. As scientists and philosophers long for answers to life, they cannot account for the fact that we are created with souls. Complicated science cannot explain conscience and our desire to acknowledge a higher being.

To put it simply, we are making a fundamental mistake. We have replaced God with mortal man, and in doing so, have made ourselves more and more ignorant. We try desperately to explain everything in terms we can understand with logical outcomes. We will continue to fail until we finally accept that we cannot completely understand everything around us and instead acknowledge the omnipotent, immortal God.

Our lack of faith and demand for proof only takes us deeper and deeper into our own stupidity. So many people think that they have all the answers to life and its problems, yet are destined to fail. Everywhere you turn someone is saying they have the answers to your problems. There is only one answer, and it lies with our belief and acceptance of our immortal God.

Faith in God comes from acceptance, faith, and dependence, which are not the solutions that the philosophers would have you believe. Enlightenment or ignorance is your choice. Faith in God or trust in today's secular explanations are the paths you can choose. Trust in God's perfect promises or dependence on the world's failures will be your results. The answers to life rest in one place, the immortal God. Place your trust in Him!

"Trust wholeheartedly in God,
Put no faith in your own perception."

PROVERBS 3:5

OUR SHEPHERD

"And when He saw the crowds He felt sorry for them because they were harassed and dejected, like sheep without a shepherd."

MATTHEW 9:36

Confused. Powerless. Under fire. Sad. Lonely. Aimless. Marginalized. Anxious. A world without a shepherd is a victim of itself as it wallows in selfishness and in the pursuit of power. A world without THE SHEPHERD is lost. We should express every ounce of gratitude in our souls that we have the Good Shepherd who has saved us, loves us, and always provides. A world with Jesus tending the flock has the promise of salvation always ahead of it as it depends on His grace to see us through.

Why does it seem like everyone disagrees about everything? Have we pushed God away? Why does it seem that we are always in a fight? Have we pushed God away? How can our leaders fail us time after time, never coming through with what they promise? Have we pushed God away?

A life without a shepherd is one of chaos and hopelessness. A life with Jesus is one of promise and hope. A life without a shepherd is one of conflict and despair. A life with Jesus is one of personal peace and mercy. A life without a shepherd is scattered and disordered. A life with Jesus is sure and compassionate. Jesus is the Good Shepherd.

Jesus is our comfort when we hurt and our companion when we feel alone. He is our guide when we are lost and our foundation when we fall. He is compassion, He is grace, and He is love. No matter what is going on in the world around us, He is always close at hand, providing us with the peace that only He can provide. Let Him lead you. Let Him shepherd you. Let Him rule you. He is the Good Shepherd who has only love for you in His heart and we can thrive when we are obedient to Him. Follow THE SHEPHERD, and find rest in Him.

*"The fear of God leads to life,
a man has food and shelter, and no evil to fear."*

PROVERBS 19:23

PSALM 4

Verse 1

Verses 8

"God, guardian of my rights, You answer when I call,
   When I am in trouble, You come to my relief.
      Now be good to me and hear my prayer."

"In peace I lie down, and fall asleep at once,
   Since You alone, God, make me rest secure."

MY FOCUS

HIS WORK OF ART

"We are God's work of art, created in Christ Jesus to live the good life as from the beginning He had meant us to live it."

EPHESIANS 2:10

Have you ever thought of yourself as a created masterpiece? Have you realized your uniqueness and individual gifts? Do you have a full appreciation for the fact that God created you just like you are, exactly for His purpose, fully capable through faith of living out the life you were intended to live? Each of us bears the handprint of the Creator, brought to fullness by the works of Christ. Our mind and body are designed with intention, lovingly formed and purposefully meant for a full life of faith in Christ. There is nothing accidental or random about us. We are special, unique, and loved by God.

The new life that we receive through faith in Christ is exactly the purpose fulfilled by God. He created us with a purpose, His purpose. He saved us for a purpose, His purpose. Through Christ we can live the life of freedom found only in Him, for His purpose. The ordinary life becomes the good life when it is centered, focused, and committed to Christ. The ordinary life becomes the good life when we allow ourselves to be open to His purpose instead of our own. He is the creator of you.

Whenever you feel down and worn out, remember that you are the masterpiece of God. Exactly as you are is exactly how He intended you to be. As you are, through Christ, the good life is yours. As you are, through Christ, you can live with an eternal focus. He had a design, a plan, an intention, and a path in mind for each of us. Too often we forget that His creative hand is always upon us and that His peace and the good life were always ours for the believing. The good life is the life created through Christ. We often think of creation as what is around us instead of remembering that each of us is the product of a loving God. Always for a purpose. Always loved. Always for relationship.

A work of art has character and love at its core. Let Christ be part of your character and at the core of your heart. A work of art has passion and intention. Let Christ bring your passion for life and your purpose to love to the forefront of your everyday approach to life. A work of art has commitment and detail. Let the commitment that Christ has to you be the reason that you call Him Lord, thank Him always, and love without boundary.

We all have value to God. Never let the world undervalue you. You are worth everything to God. You are a work of art, designed and made by the Almighty God. Believe and have faith in the power of Christ, and the good life of service to Him awaits. It is what He always intended.

*"From everlasting I was firmly set,
From the beginning, before earth came into being."*

PROVERBS 8:23

BEWARE THE THORNS

"As for the part that fell into the thorns, this is people who have heard, but as they go on their way they are choked by the worries and riches and pleasures of life and do not reach maturity."

LUKE 8:14

Does life get in the way of you becoming a mature Christian? Do the struggles of everyday life produce a worry that is greater than faith and trust in God? Do the desires for an easier life pull you away from a reliance on God? Does the adolescent level of your faith search for God for your own relief under pressure, or do you depend on God in every situation? Can you see through the trials and temptations of this world to see God in all His glory actively loving you?

These questions are difficult. Every single person has faced questions like these. Sadly, we'll face them time and again throughout the course of life. Three things will always be true: (1) you will face struggles and temptations, (2) you are not alone in your struggles, and (3) God is always there to love us in those struggles and temptations.

The big challenge for the Christian is to not let the trials of life keep us from our passion for Christ. We need to move forward in our faith and not let ourselves get bogged down by circumstances or inappropriately placed desires. Every person faces times of inadequacy, hardship, and anxiety. Every person has times of fear, loneliness, and doubt. But the good news is those same people also have a God greater than all those challenges. We have a God of victory. He is bigger than what faces you today and can lead you personally through what you will face tomorrow.

Thorns grow among the crop when it is not routinely, carefully, and purposefully attended. Are you neglecting the soil of your life, or are you continually preparing the soil to enable rich growth to let your crop bring forth the abundance intended? Does your life feel choked out by outside influences, or are you giving your soil the room it needs for your faith to prosper? What are the thorns in your life that prevent the plant from bearing its full fruit? Put your thorns in perspective and let your eyes always be fixed ahead on God.

We have seeds of the Good News. Through Christ we are true heirs of the Kingdom of Heaven. We have the ability to bear fruit beyond our imagination as we grow in deeper and deeper communion with Him. The seed is pure and mighty, given freely and trustworthy, abundant and faithful. The weeds and thorns may be all around us, but the seed will prevail to eternity. Do not let the thorns of this world choke out the promises of the Word of God in your life. Keep growing!

> *"What the wicked man fears overtakes him,*
> *What the virtuous desires comes to him as a present."*

PROVERBS 10:24

ONLY THE BELIEVER

"Who can overcome the world? Only the man who believes that Jesus is the Son of God."

1 JOHN 5:5

What does it really mean to believe in Jesus? It means I have overcome this world through faith. It means the world has no power over me. It means that the world's values do not control me. It means that the world cannot give me the peace that only God can give. It means that I am a child of God.

We are pulled and pushed by a world that is in constant turmoil. At every turn, the world tries to influence your behavior. We have let the world dictate the way we dress, the way we talk, and the way we act. We have let the world define the fruits of the Spirit as signs of weakness instead of strength. We have let the world move society away from God at a time when we need Him most. But despite the problems and issues of the day, God is never far away from the person who believes. It is through Jesus that we overcome the world, and we do it on His terms, not the world's.

If you really believe that Jesus is the Son of God, you can live forgiven. You trust in the Word and rely on faith. You know Jesus suffered, died, and rose again for you personally and for a world in need. We know that God loves us, despite ourselves, as we are, where we are. We know that because He is love, we are free to love others in every circumstance. We know we are not a slave to this world, but instead are free to give Him the praise He deserves. We know life eternal with Him awaits. The peace that passes all understanding is ours for the believing.

Only the person who believes will trust enough to let God be God. They will let Jesus live in their heart and be part of their being. They will accept Jesus as the Master of their life. They will let their life be a constant prayer doing good at every opportunity. They will put aside themselves for the sake of Jesus. Only the believer.

You cannot overcome the world on your own. You don't need to. Jesus already has. Through faith you have too. Live like it.

"Keep my principles and you will live,
Keep my teaching as the apple of your eye."

PROVERBS 7:2

OPPORTUNITY TO BE SAVED

"Think of your Lord's patience as your opportunity to be saved..."

2 PETER 3:15

How much time do you have left? How much more patience does God have with you? To so many of us it seems like we have all the time we want. The sun continues to rise in the morning and we awake from our sleep each day. The problems that were there yesterday will be there again tomorrow. Procrastination turns into complacency and lack of urgency turns into unimportance.

How would you live your last day if you knew God's patience was ending? Would God find you at peace, complete in the joy and expectation of the fulfillment of His promises? Or would He find you unprepared and focused on your priorities instead of God's? Time is a gift from God. It gives us the opportunity to prepare to be saved and to do what is necessary to live our lives every minute as a child of God. It gives us the chance to repent and the chance to enjoy the peace of His forgiveness. It gives us the chance to align our lives to the pattern and commands that God expects. It allows us the ability to live a committed, faithful, and dedicated life.

How long will the Lord's patience continue? How many more chances do you have to truly accept Him as your Lord and Savior? How many more?

No one knows but the Father, but He has told us that His time will come. There is no doubt He has lovingly shown us more patience than we deserve. Use your time wisely! The time is now to change our thinking of time. Our time here on earth will not go on forever, and it may end sooner than we can imagine. What will you do in the meantime? Time is a gift from God. How will you use it? Will our time here be cherished or wanted? His patience is our opportunity to be saved.

> *"How long do you intend to lie then, idler?*
> *When are you going to rise from your sleep?"*
>
> PROVERBS 6:9

NO NEED TO BE ANXIOUS

"Cast all your anxiety on Him because He cares for you."

1 PETER 5:7

Peace is the emotion we all desire. How do you find it? Why does peace elude us? Why don't we trust God's power? What a great blessing this verse is. We can lay our anxiety with confidence directly on God and know that our concerns are heard. What possible good can come from worry? Do we trust God to see us through our problems? Can we say with confidence that God will provide answers for us? Because He cares, we can find rest in Him.

How selfish we are when we take God out of our decisions. We think we have the answers and we can rationalize or think our way out of our problems. The shortness of our vision falls short of the care of God. Because He loves, we can have His peace.

Trust the Lord! He cares for us! Clear your mind of worries. Take yourself out of the equation of solving problems and let God provide your answer. So many times we are so busy worrying that we don't take the time to listen to the answers to our prayers. It is a great act of faith to turn over our anxieties to the Lord. God has a plan for us much greater than our eyes can see. We should not be surprised when problems occur, but instead greet them with confidence and peace. Nothing is so important as to change our focus on God. Keep your eyes on God first. We should be confident in God to listen and care. We should be at peace with the knowledge that God is an active part of our daily life. Stop carrying the burden of anxiety and live today in peace.

Do circumstances determine your actions, or does your trust in God help you persevere through difficult circumstances? Our best chances to witness are when we are facing difficult times. It is when we are stressed that the foundations of our beliefs are displayed. See how successful you can be at removing worry and anxiety from your life today. God's peace is yours.

"When the storm is over, the wicked man is no more,
but the virtuous stands firm forever."

PROVERBS 10:25

HE HAS CONQUERED

"I have told you all this so that you may find peace in me.
In the world you will have trouble, but be brave:
I have conquered the world."

JOHN 16:33

We do not have to look far to see that we live in a world that is desperate for peace. There is conflict among nations, families, individuals, and communities. Turmoil and adversity seem to be constantly challenging our abilities to cope in a sinful world. We live in a divisive time that focuses on division rather than unity, power rather than truth, and self rather than sacrifice. As society pushes God away, it seems as though the suffering in this world grows at an exponential rate. This is a world full of trouble.

Where do we look for peace? Will a new law or directive lead us to true peace? No. Will a new elected official finally bring this world together in peace? No. Will the newest role model or self-help book lead us to peace? No. There is no peace without Jesus.

We can find peace in Jesus. He has won you freedom from the cost of your sins. He has won this peace for you, individually. He has showered His grace upon us, forgiving both our original and earned sin. He lets you live free, always in His presence and always in His love. We are won by His grace, completely and for eternity. In Him we can have true peace. This is an eternal peace, not a worldly peace. This is a freedom of the heart, not a freedom of circumstances. This is joy, hope, and trust. This is peace not in yourself or anyone else, but it is peace resting completely on the love in Him.

Be brave. There is no need to worry about what really matters. When you see the world around you in chaos, rest firmly on His truth. When you think things cannot get any worse, know that He has a plan and is always in charge. When you doubt, have confidence in Him. When it seems there is nowhere to turn, know He is always with you.

Too often we forget that Jesus has already won the battle for eternity. We get so wrapped up in the present, that we forget about eternity. Nothing that happens to us here on earth can change the promises of God. We are His. We are on the winning side. We share the victory. We can rest in His grace.

The world, as it presents itself, is not a surprise to God. He has not been fooled. He is not in a panic. Jesus knew that the world would be full of trouble, and He calls us to stay firm in Him always. Do not let the challenges of the world overpower your dependence and trust in Him. His love does not change and His victory will always be. Peace is a state of spiritual rest in God. Let His mercy and grace flood your heart with His peace, no matter what is going on in your life. Honor God by believing that His peace is yours. He has conquered the world!

> *"Better a dry rust and with it peace,*
> *Than a house where feast and dispute go together."*
>
> **PROVERBS 17:1**

PSALM 63

Verses 3-8

"Your love is better than life itself,

My lips will recite Your praise;

All my life I will bless You, in Your name lift up my hands;

My soul will feast most richly, on my lips a song of joy and,

in my mouth, praise.

On my bed I think of You, I meditate on You all night long,

For You have always helped me.

I sing for joy in the shadow of Your wings;

My soul clings close to You,

Your right hand supports me."

MY FOCUS

NOT ASHAMED

"For I am not ashamed of the Good News: it is the power of God saving all who have faith—Jews first, but Greeks as well."

ROMANS 1:16

God has the power to save each of us…and He has. All believers have access to the amazing power and grace of God…ALL believers. We as individuals do not have the power or the means to earn our own salvation. It is only through faith in Christ that we can find restoration, grace, and justification by way of the power of God. It is His grace that saves.

In this verse Paul was speaking to the church in Rome. It is a pretty safe bet that believing in Christ was not the most popular position for the Romans. Preaching a new truth and a new way to salvation contrary to the society put Paul in a precarious position. It would have been easy to fade into the background and be timid in his faith, yet Paul preached with conviction and assuredness. Paul knew the truth about Jesus. He believed it completely and was willing to proclaim that belief with no reservation in order to bring more people to faith in Christ. He stood firm. He stood out in the crowd. He was proud of his faith. Do you do the same?

It seems that everywhere you look in today's society people are struggling for power. They choose position and priority over faith and humbleness. They choose to admire people in position rather than surrender their life to Jesus. They let society push God further and further away, letting intimidation by non-believers push the agenda of the world. Believers are ridiculed and overlooked, dismissed and despised. The power they seek eludes them and their search for wholeness is never-ending because they are constantly looking in the wrong places. Paul declares that it is God's power that is the answer, and only God's power can save. Faith makes it true. Faith makes it complete. Faith makes it possible. What do you believe in?

Only God's power can provide the righteousness possible for our salvation. Only God's power can provide the reconciliation we so desperately need. Only God's power can give us peace and rest in His grace.

Paul was not ashamed to declare the Good News of Jesus Christ. He stood his ground in hard situations and changed history. Against the odds that he faced, he never backed down from acknowledging the power of God to save and the importance of faith to our eternity. Paul preached the Good News to everyone, knowing that salvation was for everyone, knowing that faith was the requirement.

Let us be encouraged by the example of how Paul testified to the truth of the power of God to save. Let us rest firm on a foundation of faith in Christ and His power to bring us to salvation. Let us live boldly for Christ, unashamed and honest, proclaiming God's grace and power.

> *"For the man who finds me finds life,*
> *He will win favor from God."*
>
> **PROVERBS 8:35**

LIVE FOR HIM

"...and the reason He died for all was so that living men should live no longer for themselves, but for Him who died and was raised to life for them."

2 CORINTHIANS 5:15

Who do you live for? What portion of your day do you spend living for Christ? This verse tells you exactly who you should be living for. No greater gift could be given to you than the sacrifice of our Lord Jesus Christ. Has His gift made a difference to you?

This verse tells you to *live* for Christ, not just exist. *Live* is an active word. It means that you can use your life to emphasize the meaning of Christ's great sacrifice to others. It means you can stop looking at yourself for meaning and instead lead your life as one who is the recipient of eternal life with God. It means that the pettiness and selfishness that dominates so much of your life can be replaced with the promises of God. It means recognizing the opportunities around you every single day to further the Kingdom of God. It means acknowledging the power and deity of God.

What a difference you could make if you truly focused on living for Christ instead of yourself on a moment-by-moment basis. Everything would have a different priority and importance. Keeping Christ at the forefront of your thinking takes effort and attitude, prayer and dedication. So many things can distract you or convince you to focus on yourself. The world wants you in control of yourself. Stop and look at the decisions you make and why you make them. Do you live your life for yourself or for Christ?

With God's help, you can make the change to live for Him, finding rest and contentment in His love. He died for you. Live for Him.

"There is a way that some think right,
but it leads in the end to death."

PROVERBS 14:12

DO NOT WORRY

*"There is no need to worry; but if there is anything you need,
pray for it, asking God for it with prayer and thanksgiving, and that
peace of God, which is so much greater than we can understand,
will guard your hearts and your thoughts, in Christ Jesus."*

PHILIPPIANS 4:6-7

What great comfort this verse gives. There is no need to be anxious about anything. We can bring our concerns, no matter how big or how small, to the feet of the Father. This verse tells us we must trust in the Lord to bring peace to our hearts and minds in all situations. Worry only gets in the way of trusting and honoring God. Worrying changes the focus of our concerns to ourselves and how we can get our problems resolved by our own doing.

God is so much greater than we are! We can bring every concern to Him and know that in Christ Jesus our thoughts and hearts will be guarded. We are not left alone to fend for ourselves. We have a loving Creator who provides us with true peace. God wants us to communicate with Him on a continuous basis. He wants us to bring our concerns before Him.

Notice that this verse tells us to bring our concerns before Him with thanksgiving! We have been blessed in so many ways and are the recipients of

His promises through grace. How thankful we should be! Trust that God will provide you with His peace and thank Him continually for all the blessings that you have. This will focus your thoughts on God. God's peace is indeed greater than we can ever understand. We can be given His peace under every circumstance.

How much time do you spend worrying? Has it ever done any good? Can you turn your concerns over to God and trust Him to give you peace? Pray today with thanksgiving to God about your concerns, then accept His promise to guard your heart and thoughts. Peace can be yours.

*"Commend what you do to God,
and your plans will find achievement."*

PROVERBS 16:3

LIVE IN THE TRUTH

"It was a great joy to me when some brothers came and told of your faithfulness to the truth, and of your life in the truth."

3 JOHN 3

Joy is a state of being, dependent on faith, not circumstances. Joy comes from knowing that the assurances from God are real, dependable, and the truth. Joy is living a life full of confidence in things that go beyond our understanding. Joy is more than happiness. Joy is living with the expectation that God's Word is truth. Joy is accepting God's path, instead of our own, as our way to an eternal relationship with Him.

Faithfulness is the commitment of a servant's heart to God. It is staying true to principles that may require humbleness, but lead to intimacy with God. Faithfulness does not concern itself with quick fixes, but holds fast to the truths and promises of eternity. Faithfulness is the willingness to view life as something bigger than ourselves and to do what is right and true in all situations.

Notice that this verse not only talks about the commitment, but also the actions that confirm that commitment. It is one thing to think about real truth, and another thing to live in the real truth. This is the true test of commitment. It is what we do that reveals the level of belief we have. It is what we do when no one is watching that reveals the character of our soul. Too many of us want to think our way to salvation, doing just enough to make ourselves feel good about our actions. This is not what God wants. He wants the entire you, body and soul. He wants you to stop doing the minimum and commit, totally. He provides us with daily situations and opportunities to put our faithfulness to the truth into action.

Today, and every day, you are faced with choices. How will you respond? Let truth consume your spirit. Let it dictate your mind and put the truth into practice in everything that you do. It is through living this truth that the joy of faithfulness can be truly and completely recognized. Do you try to dwell in Him, or do you let Him dwell in you? Let your life reveal the answer to this question. It is what true joy in faithfulness is all about.

"Happy those who keep my ways."

PROVERBS 8:32B

WORRIES OF THE WORLD

"...but the worries of this world, the lure of riches and all the other passions come in to choke the word, and so it produces nothing."

MARK 4:19

More. Faster. Now. We live in a society of bountiful resources, yet the fruit it yields is withered and scant. We live in a time of anxiousness and distrust, being let down by the promises of the world. We expect politicians and laws to usher in peace and prosperity, yet all we get is division and argument. We worry over finances, worrying about how much is enough, yet are surrounded by the plight and suffering of those in need. Everything is focused on self, getting ahead, and satisfying our desires as we push God further and further away. We declare that church and state must be separated by discounting God and therefore suffer at the hands of man. We have allowed no room for God and have let all our worries and desires take our attention, reverence, and honor of God from our lives. We are choking out the word.

Where is the fruit? What are we producing that has eternal value? Where is the Word in your list of priorities? How do we put our love for God and our love for others ahead of ourselves in a world that is self-serving? Worry and anxiousness are not the fruits of faith. Ego and self-reliance do not give proper honor to our creator. The drive for more and more personal gain does not reflect the heart of the believer. Why are we choking out the Word of God?

The fruit we each bear tells us about our priorities. We can let the world choke out God, or we can bear the fruit of the Spirit. What kind of soil are you when the seed of God gets planted? Watch out for the thorns that choke out God and instead watch as you put the Word into action in your lives as it produces love, joy, peace, and patience. As self-control and gentleness rule your heart, let God clear a pathway to faithfulness. Be brave enough to walk upon that path when He does. Let nothing get in your way toward kindness and compassion. Live a life in pursuit of faith, not money. Choose to trust, not doubt. Make obedience your lifestyle and avoid the snares of false freedom. Most of all, chose to honor God, not the world of men.

The fruit we can bear focused on God can stand out in a world that has forgotten God. We are His fruit. It is up to us to clear our path toward Him and produce the fruits found only in Him.

> *"Worry makes a man's heart heavy,*
> *A kindly word makes it glad."*

PROVERBS 12:25

HE CAN TELL

*"He never needed evidence about any man;
He could tell what a man had in him."*

JOHN 2:25

Jesus knew exactly what was inside every person. He knew their motives and their weaknesses. He knew their motivation and their hearts. He knew that there were many who wanted miracles and signs and wonders but did not want to acknowledge who Jesus really was.

Much like that time many years ago, there are many who say they are believers because they want a shortcut to a miracle. We call on Jesus in times of trouble but have not worshipped Him at all times. We are long on requests and short on thanks. We too often seek God for selfish reasons and miss out on the relationship with God that brings true peace. Do you ask from God or give yourself to Him? He can tell.

The religious leaders of His day liked to put themselves above the rest. They put on shows and pageantry, relying on ceremony and edicts to prove their relationship to God. They flouted piety and wisdom while at the same time having misguided hearts. They had power and influence, yet had missed out on the real power of sacrifice and love. Many of us are like that today. They relied on Law. Jesus relies on love. He can tell.

God cannot be fooled. There is no behavior or secret He does not already know. He looks at the heart. He looks at love. He looks at our inside, while we try to polish up our outside. We desperately try to hide the flaws and project an image, but ignore our heart. What is really our motivation? He can tell.

Jesus knew the strength and weakness, conviction and apathy, admiration and selfishness in everyone. He knew the entire person, beyond what they tried to portray as truth. He knows all of us, completely. This can be a very scary thought, knowing that God sees through our facades. We cannot fool God, despite our best efforts. The good news is He loves each of us, despite our weaknesses, completely. Our evidence may be flawed, but He knows He is in us. His love is in us. His patience is in us. His mercy is in us. His power is in us. Through faith we can enjoy all these gifts and let the evidence we have be pure and compassionate. When we seek a relationship with Him first, He can tell. When we let God be God, He can tell. When we put Him above all things, He can tell. When we love without motive, He can tell.

In a world that surrounds us with the importance of image, it is very difficult to put self aside. God created each of us as unique testaments to His love, purposefully and distinct. He does not want us to be different than what He meant us to be. He knows our inside. He knows our mind. The evidence of His love is you. Live freely, knowing you do not need to prove anything to God. He can tell.

> *"As no two faces are ever alike,*
> *Unlike, too, are the hearts of men."*
>
> **PROVERBS 27:19**

PSALM 37

Verses 23-24
Verses 27-28

"God guides a man's steps,
They are sure, and he takes pleasure in his progress;
He may fall, but never fatally,
Since God supports him by the hand."

"Never yield to evil, practice good
And you will have an everlasting home,
For God loves what is right,
And never deserts the devout."

MY FOCUS

MUCH IS EXPECTED

"You always have the most of everything—of faith, of eloquence, of understanding, of keenness for any cause, and the biggest share of our affection—so we expect you to put the most into this work of mercy too."

2 CORINTHIANS 8:7

These words of Paul to the Corinthians should feel as if they were directed squarely at us. We have so much, yet we take so much for granted. We have access to the tools to do God's work, yet we fail to see the opportunities in front of us. The gift of God's blessings is ours, yet we hesitate to be full partners in His works of mercy.

Paul's expectation of the most from us is a very personal challenge. What are you doing with the faith and prosperity that God has so graciously poured onto you? We have so much of everything, far in excess of what we truly need. You do not need everything that your jealous eye tells you to lust for. Whatever faith God provides you, use it to do His works of mercy. Whatever your position and possessions, find ways to use them in all humbleness to further the kingdom of God.

You have a gift of conscience, knowing what is truly the right thing to do. Listen and be sensitive to the situations around you that cry out for the use of your gifts for the benefit of others. God has blessed you with more than you really need so that you can be partners with Him to fulfill the needs of others here on earth. God sees how you use your gifts as an indicator of what you place your trust in. Do you really think you are solely responsible for your gifts, or are you a steward of the gifts God has given you? The importance that you place in yourself and your things reveal much about your level of reliance on God.

God gives you gifts, expecting you to use them for His purposes. Be generous, be full of mercy, and be ready to use God's blessings. Treat your gifts with the honor they deserve. These gifts are truly a blessing because we have the ability to use them to benefit others over and over again. His gifts do not expire, break, or become obsolete. His gifts are part of your soul. Praise God that you have the ability and duty to share His gifts. He has given much and has every right to expect that His gifts be used for His purposes. God's gifts are truly the gifts that keep on giving. Be as good a giver as you are a receiver. His mission of mercy is waiting for your contribution.

> *"The man who is kind to the poor lends to God,*
> *he will repay him for what he has done."*

PROVERBS 19:17

FORGIVE

"Bear with one another; forgive each other as soon as a quarrel begins. The Lord has forgiven you; now you must do the same."

COLOSSIANS 3:13

Patience. Humility. Understanding. Sacrifice. All these traits are necessary to forgive someone. All of these traits were gloriously displayed by Christ. Are these traits what you consistently display?

This verse tells you what the state of your mind should be when you deal with others. You are to bear with one another. Do your best to understand a difference of opinion and realize the shortcomings of others. Be prepared to forgive. Be diligent about not getting into a situation that might cause a quarrel. As soon as you recognize conflict, obligate yourself to end it.

Forgiveness does not hold a grudge. Forgiveness does not have strings attached. How blessed you are that the Lord forgives you for the multitude of your sins. If you can be forgiven, surely you must be able to forgive. There is not much tolerance or forgiveness in the world we live in. We want to litigate and assure our "rights" at all costs. How different life would be in a world focused on forgiveness!!

Be willing to sacrifice something of yourself for your fellow man. Understand their feelings and position. Do not demand your rights, but in humility be willing to listen with patience. Just imagine how you can glorify God by your spirit of forgiveness. God is patient. Christ humbled Himself on earth to be our sacrifice. God understands our needs, desires, and shortcomings. And maybe, best of all, He forgives. Live like a forgiven person and follow His example and forgive.

> *"Do not say, 'I will repay evil', put your hope in God and He will keep you safe."*
>
> PROVERBS 20:22

AUTHORITY

"Jesus had now finished what He wanted to say, and His teachings made a deep impression on the people because He taught them with authority, and not like their own scribes."

MATTHEW 7:28-29

God's teachings are not a competing idea or simply another point of view. God is not a concept or theory that is on par with the world that we live in. God is above all things, and we need to accept and acknowledge His power and authority. His Word has authority over creation and life, morality and mortality, compassion and integrity. His Word is what we can depend on, absolute truth. His Word stands above all our own ideas and rationalizations. His Word is our authority.

Sadly, it's not uncommon to think that God has no more power than the world, that the world and God are in some kind of battle whose winner is yet to be determined. How foolish we are! The world's word is full of hypocrisy and opportunism and is based on an ever-changing concept of relativism. The world holds no absolute truth and believes that truth can only be seen from each individual's perspective. Right and wrong become subjective and right living becomes defined by individual perceptions. The world tells us to trust ourselves and does not honor the authority of God. The more authority the world tries to demand, the less authority it has. A world without God and His authority will fail.

The good news is that God is in control. He alone is the true authority of our lives. In Him is absolute truth, peace, and joy. His rewards are eternal and the impact of His authority on our lives is transformative. His promises do not change, and we can depend not on ourselves, but on His justice and compassion for all eternity. His Word and teachings are not just another book for our consideration. His Word should consume us as we realize the importance of His will at work in our day-to-day. It is time we give His Word the reverence and honor it deserves.

What impresses you? Is it the promises of the world or of God? Can you declare that there is power in His Word and that it is the basis for how you live your life every day, in every situation? Do you trust His teachings to be the absolute truth? His Word is not like anything else in the world. It has the authority of God Himself and contains the power to touch each of our souls. Cherish His gift to you and make it the central part of your faith. May the Word of God make a deep impression on you as you listen, obey, and honor His authority.

"He who listens closely to the Word shall find happiness,
He who puts his trust in God is blessed."

PROVERBS 16:20

LAVISHED IN LOVE

> *"Think of the love that the Father has lavished on us, by letting us be called God's children; and that is what we are. Because the world refused to acknowledge Him, therefore it does not acknowledge us."*

1 JOHN 3:1

As part of the nature of God, He is abundant, complete, and generous. His is a love that gives to overflowing, is extravagant in its fullness, and is overpowering with its compassion and sincerity. There are no limits to His grace and no boundaries to His mercy. We are the object of His love and made righteous through faith in Him because of His mercy. He showers us with love. He covers us with His care.

We need to remind ourselves just how important and loved each one of us is in His eyes. He has given us His very best gift, making us his children. Think about how that changes everything. We can move past knowing about God to a place where we experience God Himself. We can live every day with a thankful, joyous heart knowing that we belong in His family. We can devote more time to thanksgiving, knowing our future is secure and we are always loved. We can live with a peaceful heart no matter what the circumstances because our Father is powerful, generous, and patient. We can let our lives be a daily worship to our creator, our sustainer, and our reason to love. Think and be thankful.

Imagine waking up every morning with a thankful heart. Imagine leading a daily life full of faithful confidence in everything we do. Imagine looking for ways to honor our Father through acts of love. Imagine your faith growing and growing as you depend on God and receive His love. God has given us the ultimate gift to be included in His family, because He is love, He is grace, and He is mercy. May we accept Him for who He is, our Father, and give thanks for His lavished love.

> *"Fear of God gives good grounds for confidence,*
> *In Him, His children find a refuge."*
>
> PROVERBS 14:26

CALL ON JESUS

"All who call on the name of the Lord will be saved."

ACTS 2:21

Yes, this is for even me, a sinner. I will be saved when I rely on the name of the Lord. The saving grace of Jesus is for all believers. It does not leave anyone out. These most inclusive words here are spoken by Peter at Pentecost to assure all the listeners of the absolute power and promise of Jesus. The people were used to rules and regulations, prerequisites and prejudices. People were divided by race and gender, poverty and position. There were religious obstacles and social barriers. It is just like life today.

These words are as true today as they have ever been. This verse unifies all of us under the banner of Christ. ALL…ALL…ALL who call on the Lord will be saved. We do not save ourselves by what we do or what power we may wield. We are saved only through Jesus! In the name of Jesus we are all the same, equal heirs of His grace. We are loved in spite of ourselves and we are all looked at equally as created creatures by God when we believe.

Calling on the name of Jesus is not a spell we cast. No mysticism can change our eternity. Calling on the name of Jesus may not change your circumstance, but it will change your heart. Calling on the name of Jesus is a way of life and commitment. It is an acknowledgment of the work on the cross of Jesus for our sins and sharing in the grace of eternal life in heaven because of the resurrection. It is proclaiming the power and majesty, grace and reconciliation, justification and sanctification through Jesus. It is the commitment to live a life enriched by the Spirit committed to Jesus. It is being an example of Christ as we treat others with honesty, humility, and equality. It is finding the best in our fellow man and doing our best to enrich their lives through love. His name has power. His name gives righteousness. His name saves. You. Me. Everyone who believes.

It seems that everyone is searching today. We search for answers, freedom, and justice. We read books, listen to authorities, and are told by self-help experts how to live our lives. We diet, exercise, and meditate to help our self-esteem. We look for easy answers anywhere we can find them. We spend hours searching the internet for solutions. We battle prejudices and attitudes. We search but cannot find a purpose. Look somewhere else. Everyone needs Jesus.

This one verse, in a mere 12 words, tells us all we need to know. Call on Him and you will find salvation. Call on Him and you can have a peace that passes all understanding. Call on Him and your heart can overflow in His grace. Call on Him to find rest in His promises. There is no need to look everywhere for answers. The answer has been there all the time. The answer is Jesus.

> *"The name of God is a strong tower;*
> *The virtuous man runs to it and is secure."*

PROVERBS 18:10

NO TRACE OF DOUBT

*"But he must ask with faith, and no trace of doubt,
because a person who has doubts is like waves
thrown up in the sea when the wind is driven."*

JAMES 1:6-7

How can you be so sure? By faith, we are assured. What can make you so confident? Faith assures us. How can you possibly believe something you cannot prove? It is by faith we can have assurance. A series of tough questions that have what seems to be a simple answer. Can it be that simple? Yes. A person of faith is unshakeable, knowing that true joy is eternal. There is no doubt. A person of faith looks beyond themselves and trusts God to be the ultimate answer. A person of faith knows that Christ's sacrifice has opened the door to eternity in heaven.

One of the consistent themes throughout the New Testament is our constant struggle for explanations of things we cannot know and our insistence on placing emphasis on the temporary while ignoring the eternal. It is our doubt that continues to plague us and muddy the message of faith in Jesus Christ. He has done all that is necessary, despite our failings. We want to earn a place in heaven, while He wants a relationship, a trusting, faithful relationship. Eternity is ours for the believing. Anxiousness can disappear when it is God we trust instead of ourselves. Peace, true peace, and contentment can be found when we value His promise and His sacrifice instead of our selfish demands.

Everything around us is full of doubt. Nothing seems to be as it appears. Rationalizations and relativism attack even the most basic moral absolutes. We are pulled in many directions at the same time, confused by contradictory ideas. We are a society that is truly being blown around by winds of intellectual perceptions like a wispy morning mist.

It is only with faith that we can find a true foundation to weather the storms of life. God stands firm in His righteousness, forgiveness, and strength. He is there, waiting for us to come to Him in faith. What is stopping us? Isn't it time that we confidently, assuredly profess our eternal destiny is assured? In faith there can be doubt.

> *"Trust wholeheartedly in God,*
> *Put no faith in your own perceptions."*

PROVERBS 3:3

PSALM 25

Verses 4-5

Verses 10-11

"God, make Your ways known to me,
Teach me Your paths.
Set me in the way of Your truth, and teach me,
For You are the God who saves me."

"All God's paths are love and truth
For those who keep His covenant and His decrees.
For the sake of Your name, God,
Forgive my guilt, for it is great."

MY FOCUS

KEEP YOUR EYES ON JESUS

> *"Let us not lose sight of Jesus, who leads us in our faith and brings it to perfection: for the sake of the joy which was still in the future, He endured the cross, disregarding the shamefulness of it, and from now on has taken His place at the right of God's throne."*
>
> HEBREWS 12:2

For the sake of our joy, Jesus endured. For the sake of our joy, Jesus suffered, died, and rose again victorious to assure our eternity. For the sake of our joy, Jesus overwhelmed evil. Through faith, He delivers us. With our eyes always on Jesus, the entire world changes. With our eyes on Jesus, we sacrifice and love without hesitation, just as He loved us. With our eyes on Jesus, we can experience real joy, completely engulfed in the reality of His love for each of us. Happiness is something we strive for, but joy is the lasting gift from God.

In a Facebook post, Kay Warren has described the joy we have with Jesus this way: "Joy is the settled assurance that God is in control of all the details of my life, the quiet confidence that ultimately everything is going to be alright, and the determined choice to praise God in all things." This is a wonderful definition, but only given real meaning if we believe it. Jesus is the only one who can bring our faith to perfection. Jesus is the only one sitting at the right hand of God. Jesus is the only one whose sacrifice was sufficient to save us. Not us. Not someone else. Only Jesus.

If God is really in control of the details of our life, our need for anxiousness and worry are gone. If we think eternally, we know Christ has won the battle for our souls, and we can rest in that fact. If we have real confidence in God, then there is joy in everything. If our eyes are focused on Jesus, we can find a reason to give thanks always because we are blessed and loved always. If our eyes are on Jesus, we allow Him to guide us through faith and are able to experience real joy. Real joy is only found in one place: the love of Jesus.

We all have plenty of things in our lives that are trying to grab our attention. We sometimes let the world have power over us. Maybe it is time to change focus. Maybe it is time to see how little power the world has over us when we see things through the lens of Christ. Maybe we stop to think about how fleeting and temporary the gifts of the world are versus the real value of gifts of Jesus, our eternity and peace. Maybe it is time to keep our eyes on Jesus.

It is difficult to stay in close relationship with Jesus when we let our focus be pulled in so many directions. It is easy and frustrating to let our pursuit of worldly happiness take our energy, leaving Jesus behind. Energy spent on Jesus is never wasted. Real joy is in Jesus. We all focus on what is the most important thing at the moment. Let every moment be focused on Jesus. Real joy is in Jesus. It seems like in this world right now you cannot trust much of anything or any person. Have confidence in the real truth and the real place for trust. Real joy is in Jesus.

Instead of wanting more and more things, strive for more and more Jesus. With that effort comes the joy, the real joy, knowing that He wants nothing more than you to experience that joy deep down into your soul. Live in His victory and with His joy.

> *"The hope of all virtuous men is all joy,*
> *The expectations of the wicked are frustrated."*

PROVERBS 10:28

JUDGE WHAT IS RIGHT

"Why not judge for yourselves what is right?"

LUKE 12:57

Just think what a different world this would be if everyone just did the right thing with conviction and energy. It is easy to go along with the crowd and let ourselves be influenced into mediocrity, the easier path that takes less effort. It also lowers our expectations of both ourselves and our society. It takes energy to stand firm and relentlessly follow in the steps of Jesus, doing "what is right" at all times. It requires effort to set ourselves apart for Jesus. It takes strength to stand up to the crowd and not give up on our values, ideals, and faith. It is easy to grow tired, but it is always right to stay rooted in Jesus.

We live in a space and time where our values and faith are being challenged daily. It requires our full attention and effort to remain strong. When it comes to faith, there is no compromise. Letting sin creep closer is never the path toward Christ. Remaining vigilant and committed to the path toward Christ is something that demands our best effort and consistent attention. That path toward Jesus is the right path, and it is a road that needs to be taken, no matter what the challenges. Each of us is responsible for staying energized and alive for Christ, step by step, always striving to do "what is right." Is it always easy? No. Will it sometimes require sacrifice? Yes. Will it be the popular way? Not always. Then why do we do it? It is because He first loved us. It is the right thing to do.

When Jesus spoke these words to the crowd, He knew that they were in need of encouragement and assuredness that following Christ was the right thing to do. He wanted their hearts to be engaged in the process of doing the right thing in all the real situations of their life. Just like in those days, we as followers of Christ need to be encouraged and prodded to live under the power of the strength of Jesus. Faith is a journey. It is the most important journey we will ever undertake. It is easy to get distracted and disillusioned. However, the good news is the commitment to doing what is right is a higher calling, a calling from God Himself. Be steadfast. Be strong. Draw on the energy of Christ, knowing that His power will see us through any situation. Stay on the road to Jesus. Never give up. Never tire of doing "the right thing."

This verse also reminds us that the opportunity to support and be part of a larger effort to do the right thing is always in front of us. How can you help and guide others to the virtue of life in the Lord? How do your actions make it easier for someone to follow Jesus? How does your attitude of consistency for Christ give encouragement to someone else? How does your servant heart give worth and meaning to the journey toward Christ to another? It is up to each of us individually to stand for Jesus, but remember that your example also has the power to encourage others to stand alongside you. Let your faith radiate, encouraging others to do the right thing and commit themselves to Christ. Be strong and never tire.

*"To act virtuously and with justice
is more pleasing to God than sacrifice."*

PROVERBS 21:3

LISTEN TO THE TRUTH

> *"The time is sure to come when, far from being content with sound teaching, people will be avid for the latest novelty and collect themselves a whole series of teachings according to their own tastes, and then instead of listening to the truth, they will turn to myths."*
>
> 2 TIMOTHY 4:3-4

Why do we try so hard to make simple things so difficult? Why must everything we do be on our own terms? Why are we never content with sound teaching? We all struggle with these three areas. That struggle keeps us from simple contentment.

Acceptance. What is there about us that keeps us from simple acceptance? The mysteries of God and His promises are not to be intellectually understood. The Word has plenty of evidence, encouragement, and power to convince us what is right and what is wrong. It seems that today's society is more and more skeptical, needing evidence on its own terms to know what is true. We want no absolutes, but only relevancy. Faith is not something to be scientifically proven, but instead experienced. We are not God's equal intellectually. His plans, sacrifices, and promises may not make sense to us, but are no less real. We find it difficult to understand grace, because it is a concept that is not in our nature, only God's. We make our salvation so difficult when what God requires is so easy. The gift of salvation and righteousness is ours with our acceptance of His truths.

Obedience. For some reason, obedience unto the Lord is difficult for us. Maybe we feel that we must have a better plan than God. Perhaps we feel that we need to fine-tune God's will for us so that it better fits our own ideas of the truth. Obedience is very difficult for most of us because we have to come to terms that we are under God. It is not easy to accept the position of servitude and that compared to God, we have such limited power. God is the one to worship, not ourselves. We are to be obedient to His Word and will, not ourselves. The plan for our salvation is God's, not ours. We are to be obedient and be used as servants. The sound teachings are not given to us so that we can modify them to our own likings. The truths can become myths when we replace God's truths with a version of our own. God doesn't want our rationalizations and modifications; He desires our obedience. Through obedience we can keep truths that He has given us in a state of wholeness.

Reliance. Learning to rely on the sound teaching of God is essential. Jesus has the complete plan for each of us already in place. God's perfect plan does not need our selfish intellectual ideas added to it. Rely on His Word with complete trust. Do not be swayed by the new ideas of salvation that the world continues to put forth. All that we need is provided to us through His Word, and it is worthy of our trust and reliance. Use His truths for support, growth, and comfort. With so many earthly ideas pulling at us, only His Word can be truly relied upon.

The sound teaching of God remains and stays alive within us with our acceptance, obedience, and reliance. Do not let new age ideas take you away from the solid foundation that the Word provides.

> *"There is a way that some think right,*
> *But it leads in the end to death."*
>
> **PROVERBS 14:12**

NO LIMITS

"There is nothing I cannot master with the help of the One who gives me strength."

PHILIPPIANS 4:13

No trial that we face can overpower us when we have the strength of God in us. No temptation can sweep us away from faith when we have the strength of God in us. No future worry can steal our purpose or enthusiasm when we have the strength of God in us. The power of God will never fail us when we rely on Him in faith. Hold on to that power!

When we accept the strength of God, we acknowledge that His power far exceeds our own. We attest to the fact that we need His strength in our weakness, His presence in our loneliness, and His patience in our anxiousness. He has the power to give us rest and peace, contentment and assuredness. His power grants us understanding in times of conflict, unity in times of division, and perspective in times of panic. When we rely on God, we have access to the power of God which always wins and always provides. In His power, we are victors over death, heirs with Christ, and recipients of grace and mercy. We can live unafraid and abundantly, knowing that God is always within reach and always loving. With God as your master, all else is powerless against you.

There is power in the name of God. His presence is real and mighty, freeing us to hold tightly to Him and receive His grace. God has chosen to love us, so stay close to Him and let His power protect and guide you through every adversity and trial. Celebrate that we have a mighty God who showers us with blessings and love. With God, there are no limits. He provides so that we can live abundantly in Him.

*"Fear of God gives good grounds for confidence,
In Him, His children find a refuge."*

PROVERBS 14:23

ARE YOU SURE?

*"We can be sure that we know God
only by keeping His commandments."*

1 JOHN 2:3

All of us should be in a pursuit to move from knowing about God to knowing God, the person. We must form a personal, intimate relationship with God. Achieving that goal takes more than knowledge, it takes purposeful action. The proof of our believing in the person of God will be evident as we keep all the commandments.

Do you put God above all things? What things get in your way of seeing God's hand in everything you have, see, and do? Are you able to set yourself aside and recognize God is to be at the center of all things?

Do the words you use reflect the grace and love of God? Are your words nurturing or used for purposes to tear down? Do you hold the name of God to be sacred and powerful, setting Him above all things? Do you call on God for your own purposes, or do you seek His Name for peace and comfort that only He can provide?

Do you set time aside just for God? Can you keep the perspective that God deserves to be honored and revered and to not let Him get lost in your busy schedule? The worshipping of God is not just an exercise, it is a holy privilege.

Do you honor those who have charge over you? Respect for your father and mother is a model for the respect you show your heavenly Father.

Do you honor life and its sanctity? We are all created beings, under the care of God. We have all sinned and all deserve the same punishment, but also can be equal heirs with Christ. Life is to be celebrated, nurtured, and honored as a gift. What will you do with your life to honor God?

Has society and its temporal lures taken your attention away from God? Has a sexual culture made you forget the purity and love of God? We are drowning in a culture that glamorizes self-indulgence. Can you separate yourself?

Selfishness can steal so many things from so many people. We steal ideas, time, and physical things in an effort to elevate ourselves above others. God has provided all you need. Use what He has given you to its fullest and find contentment.

What is truth? The Christian knows that God is God, and that cannot ever be denied. There is absolute truth. Truth today has become relevant, and it is easy to fall into the false notion that there are multiple versions of it. Do not be fooled. Hold firm to what you know is true. Hold firm to God.

How much is enough? Too many of us are focused on "more," at any cost. The desires of self continually get in the way of the desires for a relationship with God. Contentment and peace can be ours if we have the heart of God.

The answers to these personal questions will tell each of us if we really know God. The commandments are not a set of rules, they are a way of life and a commitment to live as a child of God. Do you know God?

"The name of God is a strong tower;
The virtuous man runs to it and is secure."

PROVERBS 18:10

NO DISTINCTIONS

"My brothers, do not try to combine faith in Jesus Christ, our glorified Lord, with the making of distinctions between classes of people."

JAMES 2:1

Every person on this planet shares something special. We are all created beings through the purpose and power of God, all showered in the same love, mercy, and grace of God. There are no distinctions, no proportioning, and no limits to His love. There is no race or ethnicity, power or privilege, or status or position that has an advantage or monopoly on the love and mercy of God. We make a grave mistake when we try to put restrictions and prerequisites on that love. Jesus Christ came to save all of us.

We spend a lot more time looking for our differences rather than looking at what can bind us all together. Faith in the saving grace of Jesus Christ binds us all in unity around the Almighty God. God's mercy is not reserved for a few, but instead for all those who find faith in Him. Why do we let so many things divide us? Why do we not see His creative hands in every single human being? Too often we fail to appreciate that God binds us together.

Today, look for chances to see unity rather than divisiveness. Put distinctions aside and see everyone for who they are, a creation of God. Do not let people try to separate us into competing groups, but instead demand that we all be treated equally in Christ. Do whatever you can to mend broken relationships and make an effort to build peace and understanding wherever you are. We may all be different, but we all have value in the eyes of God. We all have more in common than we think. We are loved by God.

> *"Many a man seeks a ruler's favor,*
> *But the rights of each come from God."*
>
> PROVERBS 29:26

PSALM 32

Verse 5

Verse 11

"At last I admitted to You I had sinned;
No longer concealing my guilt,
I said, 'I will go to God and confess my fault'.
And You, You have forgiven the wrong I did,
Have pardoned my sin."

"Rejoice in God,
Exult, You virtuous,
Shout for joy, all upright hearts."

MY FOCUS

NEVER THIRSTY

"..but anyone who drinks the water that I shall give will never be thirsty again: the water that I shall give will turn into a spring inside him welling up to eternal life."

JOHN 4:14

Christ is the bubbling, active movement of fulfillment inside those who find their faith in Him. The nurturing source of sustenance provided by Christ never runs out and always satisfies. He is the source that provides what we need to see us through the parched times in our lives when we feel dry and fatigued. His gift of His living water can see us through when we need it the most. We thirst for a lot of things in this life and never quite seem satisfied and never feel fulfilled. Christ, however, is offering to quench our thirst in the present and in the future as He assures us of His power and life-giving grace. He never runs out. He is a God of abundance and satisfaction. Let Him fill you up to the brim. Enjoy His fullness.

Too many of us go through life with a dehydrated spirit. We search for a full life dependent on this world only to be disappointed. Christ is offering something completely different. Faith in Him swells our spirit, fills us to the brim, and lets His grace flow through us. He provides and sustains, nurtures and supports, and gives and forgives us, even through our most difficult of days. Instead of looking outward to quench your thirst, let Christ reside inside you and give you all the water you will ever need. Find satisfaction in Christ as He quenches your thirst for eternity.

> *"Deep in water are the purposes in human hearts,*
> *The discerning man has only to draw them out."*
>
> PROVERBS 20:5

CONTENTMENT

"But Godliness with contentment is great gain."

1 TIMOTHY 6:6

One of the most important personal advances we can make is to find contentment. We get so caught up in striving for more and more that we miss the fact that God has a plan for us. We are placed where we are for a purpose. Have you taken the time to look for His purpose in your circumstances? How many opportunities to witness for Christ have you missed while you are concerned about advancing yourself?

This world does not owe us anything, but we owe our lives to God. Contentment allows us the freedom to look for possibilities to be faithful to God's plan. Lack of contentment opens our natural desires to sin, leading to the damage of our souls. Confidence that God will provide changes our attitudes. We have all been given different gifts and to covet the gifts of others is sinful. Why do we keep comparing ourselves with others? Be happy with what you have, for it is God's blessing to you. It may not seem fair, but it is what God in His perfection has planned for you.

God has a purpose for you today in your present circumstances. Use the gifts He has given you. Thank God for what He has given you, and give Him the respect He deserves through your contentment. He will use you today.

Hopefully, we can all realize that our gifts come from God and our focus will change to one of godliness with contentment. Happiness and peace are the result of your contentment in Christ. Thank you, Jesus, for that blessing.

*"Drink the water from our own cistern,
fresh water from your own well."*

PROVERBS 5:15

FASTEN YOUR ATTENTION

*"Instead of giving in to your impulses like a young man,
fasten your attention on holiness, faith , love and peace, in union
with all those who call on the Lord with pure minds."*

2 PETER 2:22

Holiness is not a fleeting thought or posture; it is a goal with an eye on Christ. Faith is not wavering or temporary; it is the foundation for eternal hope and joy. Love is not something given lightly; it is a willing commitment full of mercy and grace. Peace is not just for the moment; it is the continual rest and contentment that can only be found in Christ. Be steadfast in your commitment to the fruits of faith in Christ.

We are faced with a relentless array of things that try to steal our attention. Images come at us at an ever-quickening pace. The message of "I want it all, and I want it now" pervades every corner of our society. Life comes at us faster and faster, and we become shallower and shallower. Our attention is for sale to the the most expedient bidder. It is easy to lose sight of what is really important. To what do you fasten your attention?

Peter tells us in this verse to fasten ourselves firmly to parts of our character rather than reactions. Holiness, faith, love, and peace deserve our undivided attention because they mirror the character of Christ. Those characteristics of Christ come to fruition in us when we are mature enough to prioritize them and fasten ourselves firmly to them. As we grow in our relationship with Christ, we become more firmly fixed to the source of our maturity and joy. With our attention firmly in Christ we can see God's plan for us as not a series of reactions, but as a plan with purpose and value. He wants the best fruit for us, the most meaningful relationship with Him, and the fullness of His promises worked within us. Do not let anything in this world pull you away from adhering to Christ. Fasten yourself firmly and never let go.

What gets your attention? Are you looking for opportunities to love? How is your faith revealed in your day-to-day interactions with others? Despite the short-term possible repercussions, do you focus on doing what is right in the eyes of God? Does your life reflect the confident peace that only Christ can give? We are all on a journey in life that calls out for growth and maturity in Christ. With our attention on Him we can see what is really important in life. We must fasten ourselves to the character that comes with Christ. Stick firm. It's time to hold fast and never let go.

"Commend what you do to God,
And your plans will find achievement."

PROVERBS 16:3

IS GOD LIVING IN YOU?

> *"If a man who was rich enough in the world's goods saw that one of his brothers was in need, but closed his heart to him, how could the love of God be living in him?"*
>
> 1 JOHN 3:17

If God is truly living in you, your actions will be the evidence. If you are filled with His Spirit, no opportunity to help will pass you by. When God lives in you, your life seizes the opportunities for service, sacrifice, and love. Who among us could not find some way to help our brother or sister in need? God will give you the ability and opportunity to use the goods of this world to serve His purpose.

The more we meet the needs of others, the more we grow. You can't out-give God, you can't out-serve God, and you can't out-love God. You are His tool, used to fulfill the needs of others. We can see the difference that God living in you makes in the verse. It has to do with the heart. When God is absent, the heart is closed. With God, your heart is the beacon by which your true spirit shines out into the world. If God is in you, your heart will be open and filled with compassion and empathy. Our concerns turn away from ourselves and instead focus on the needs of others. The riches of this world become tools instead of goals. The love of God reaches inside and allows us to do what is right. God's love for mankind is revealed through us by our compassionate deeds.

We are saved by grace, and we commit through deeds. Is your heart open? Is God living in you? There is a difference between believing in God and having God live in you. When God lives in you, your entire life is changed from what the world expects. Service, sacrifice, love, humility, stewardship, and peace are all words that describe a person who has God living in them. Do these words describe you? Open your heart, and be sure that there is a place for God to live. He doesn't want to visit your heart. He wants to make a home.

> *"The generous soul will prosper,*
> *he who waters, will be watered."*

> PROVERBS 11:25

BE CAREFUL HOW YOU ACT

*"Be sure, then, you are never spiteful, or deceitful, or hypocritical,
or envious and critical of each other."*

1 PETER 2:1

Wouldn't this world be a different place if we all held to these instructions? The way that we treat others says so much about our character and love for God. It shows in a transparent manner, the level of our relationship with God. It reveals our perceptions of self-interest against the incomprehensible value that God has for us.

All the traits listed in this verse are ones of selfishness and self-importance. They describe the actions of a person who puts trust in themselves instead of God. Too often, they describe us!

Leave no doubt about your motives! Let others see the love of Christ by staying away from these behaviors. It would be a good thing to ask ourselves throughout our daily routines some of these tough questions. Have we criticized anyone today, or have we taken the opportunity to compliment when we can? Have we set our standards so high for others that they are sure to fail? Do we find ways to rationalize our own behaviors to a different level? Do we envy the material things that we see others have? Or have we found peace and contentment in the situation that God has placed us?

What we should do is be sure our lives reflect the commands of this verse and realize what our behavior says about our faith. Never be spiteful or deceitful, but instead have a humble heart that values truthfulness and the honor of others. Never be hypocritical, but instead lead a transparent life that realizes we are all held to the same standard, God's standard. Never be envious, but instead celebrate the gifts that others have received and know that God has and will continue to provide us with everything that we need.

It must be God whom we trust, not ourselves. We have so many opportunities to strengthen each other's faith and should never tear each other apart. If we can commit to and accept this verse as a way of life, we will speak loudly about our God. We will reveal His peace in our lives and be able to witness to the world about the faith and trust that we put in Him. His grace and love will radiate from us to the world. The more we make our lives about serving Him and the less about ourselves, the more we display His loving, all-encompassing essence. His peace and contentment can be ours. Live it!

"The joy of the fool lies in doing wrong,
But the joy of the man of discernment is acquiring wisdom."

PROVERBS 10:23

HEART AT PEACE

*"Do not let your hearts be troubled.
Trust in God still, and trust in me."*

JOHN 14:1

Trouble is everywhere we look. Political turmoil, societal disorder, and individual difficulties are all around us. The world appears to be in a downward spiral as we search for truth in a judgmental period of time. So how can we find peace? Is it in a strong economy? NO. A new political leader? NO. A better job or a bigger house? NO. A new exercise routine or a new medical breakthrough? NO. Our hearts will always be troubled when we don't leave any room for God. Only through Him is there real peace.

No matter how bad things may appear, the promises of God and His peace that passes all understanding is never far away. We lose sight of God when all we see is trouble. We only see disappointment when we trust in ourselves instead of God. Our hearts are empty and our souls deteriorate when we push God away. When everything seems lost, God is there still, waiting. When disappointment saps our strength, the strength of God is there still, waiting. When we let trouble overwhelm our thoughts, the peace and rest that God can provide are there still, waiting. To receive what God has to offer we have to do only one thing: trust.

We trust when we believe in His grace and peace. We trust when we believe Christ suffered, died, and rose for our salvation. We trust when we live free to love in abundance to reflect His love for each of us. We trust when we are humble enough to rely on His strength to see us through troubled times. He is there to care for us always.

God is bigger than any trouble we could have. Push the trouble aside and let the peace of God come inside your heart. The love of God shown through Christ is stronger than anything, more dependable than anything, and will never go away. Trust in Him and find the peace in your heart that He intends.

"To be afraid of men is a snare,
He who puts his trust in God is secure."

PROVERBS 29:25

PSALM 31

Verses 1-3

"In You, God, I take shelter;
Never let me be disgraced.
In Your righteousness deliver me, rescue me,
Turn Your ear to me, make haste!
Be a sheltering rock for me,
A walled fortress to save me!
For You are my rock, my fortress;
For the sake of Your name, guide me, lead me!"

MY FOCUS

LET SUFFERING BE THE BEGINNING

"These sufferings bring patience, as we know, and patience brings perseverance, and perseverance brings hope, and this hope is not deceptive, because the love of God has been poured into our hearts by the Holy Spirit which has been given us."

ROMANS 5:4

Suffering needs to be looked at as merely a first step towards hope. Look at the traits that God develops in us as we allow sufferings to turn into hope. How patient are you? Are you willing to trust God enough to wait for Him? In today's society of wanting solutions faster and faster have we lost sight of the value of patience? Without patience, how can perseverance be nurtured? Perseverance lets us realize the true value of what we are searching for. Is the answer to your suffering worth waiting for? Can you persevere in all situations, or will you look for the easy answers? As believers we are able to both be patient and persevere under adverse circumstances.

More importantly, it is because of the Holy Spirit in our hearts that we know we can have faith in hope. This hope is a gift directly from God, poured into us because of His love. How differently can you handle your sufferings when you know that through it all there is hope, true hope? This hope is worth trusting in because we know we can trust in the love of God.

He has the power to give us perspective in our sufferings, the strength to be patient, the will to persevere, and the promise of hope. God gives us the whole package for peace no matter what circumstances we find ourselves in.

All of these traits serve to develop our Christian character and depth of commitment. We can look at suffering differently when we know it will serve to develop our hope and mature our faith. Nothing exposes our true feelings more than suffering. Are you a mature Christian who can suffer with patience, persevere, and do it all because you trust your hope in God? This would be a very difficult task if it were not for the love of God that this passage says has been poured into our hearts. Let suffering be the seed for your hope. God's love will give you peace.

> *"The hope of virtuous men is all joy,*
> *the expectations of the wicked are frustrated."*
>
> PROVERBS 10:28

HUMBLENESS

*"Anyone who exalts himself will be humbled,
and anyone who humbles himself will be exalted."*

MATTHEW 23:12

We are taught from an early age that being first is the goal to be achieved. Finishing second does not win you the blue ribbon or get the headlines. The trophy is held by the winner as the rest look on with envy. We make role models out of celebrities and stars, giving value to their money, prestige, and status. We live in a society where money talks and attention is given to the most outlandish behaviors and attitudes. Sensationalism is in front of us every day. Egotism rules social media as people strive to draw attention to themselves. This is not the path for the believer.

It is odd that most people see humbleness as a sign of weakness. If you are not climbing over the top of someone, you will be the footstool for others. If you forgive, you will be taken advantage of. If you are a person of faith, you are ridiculed as a myth believer and science denier. How did we as a society get so far off the message of Christ?

Humbling yourself means that you realize and recognize that there is a power greater than yourself…Jesus. Humbling yourself means that your love for others is the foundation for your decisions and actions. Humbling yourself means following the example of Jesus to put the needs of others first as you strive to serve Him. Humbling yourself means your heart is set on service, helpfulness, and love.

Fame and fortune do not have the power that God has, nor does prestige or glory. The harder we try to elevate ourselves the less dependent we become on the saving grace of God. The more we think of ourselves, the less we think about the mercy and kindness of God. The more we put pride in ourselves first, the less generous we are to those truly in need.

The only person worthy of praise, adoration, and exaltation is God. Just think what a different world this would be if we spent the time that we waste on the opinions of the world "experts" embracing the Word. How different would society be if we listened to God first and always instead of following the current trend or opinion? How different would everything be if an attitude of thanks and honor to God was at our core. It is always time to say yes to the authority and majesty of God. It is always time to give praise and honor to the power and love of God. He promises great victory for those with a humble heart. Put that heart into action and let others see that God rules you completely. Let God be God.

> *"A man's pride brings him humiliation,*
> *He who humbles himself will win honor."*
>
> PROVERBS 29:23

IMITATE GOD

"Try, then, to imitate God, as children of His that He loves, and follow Christ by loving as He loved you, giving Himself up in our place as a fragrant offering and a sacrifice to God."

EPHESIANS 5:1-2

The goal of every believer should be to become as close in nature to God as possible.

Why: Because He first loved us, while we were still sinners, to be His precious child.

How: By being a reflection of His love with the same passion that He has for each of us.

Means: By letting our lives be an offering and sacrifice to God.

These verses sum up the basis for the Christian life. We are His children, co-heirs with Christ, and the object of the love of God. As His children, we want to identify and display the most special of the traits of God, His love. His love displaces the price of our sin and replaces it with hope and joy.

The nature of God and the magnitude of His grace overwhelms our sins and lets us enjoy communion and relationship directly with the Almighty God. How blessed we are and how wonderful is He!

How do we respond? The goal of the Christian is to put that same type of love into action in our lives. Our light for Christ should shine to everyone. Every day we have ample opportunity to reflect the love of God. Paul, in this letter, is telling us to go beyond worship and to go beyond just knowing about Christ. We, too, need to be the "fragrant offering" to a world that needs to see God's love in action.

Christ's love is complete and sacrificial. His love is unselfish and full of grace. His love is pure and has no ulterior motives. His love is universal and inclusive. Can the same be said about the way we approach life? Can we imitate that kind of love in every circumstance?

Fragrance fills an entire room. Christ's fragrance is love. Christ's love and sacrifice fills and covers all of mankind and does not change. What kind of fragrance does your life reveal? What is your daily offering to God? Is it your best imitation of the love of God?

We cannot hope to imitate God's power or His majesty, but we can hope to imitate His love. We can love, because we have been loved, and continue to be loved. Christ's "fragrant sacrifice" has made that love possible and evident. The world gives us plenty of examples of what to imitate, none of which recognize that we are children of God. We need to look no further than Christ to see who is really worthy of imitation. Christ is all we need. Let His love be the object of your attention and the example by which you live.

"Fragrant oil gladdens the heart,
Friendship's sweetness comforts the soul."

PROVERBS 27:9

HE WILL NOT DESERT YOU

"Put greed out of your lives and be content with whatever you have;
God Himself has said: I will not fail you or desert you,
and so we can say with confidence:
With the Lord to help me, I fear nothing:
what can man do to me?"

HEBREWS 13:5-6

How does a life without fear sound? Better yet, how about a life full of confidence? Best of all, how about a loving Father who will never fail you? These are the promises of God. What a great sense of security and peace this verse gives!

What are you afraid of? Are you afraid of losing your possessions, your money, and your place in society? More importantly, are you afraid of losing your soul? This verse is one of triumph! Do not fear anything! What harm can possibly be worth fearing when the Lord is there to help you.

You are a saved child of God, and you need to start living like one. Live in peace, joy, and thanksgiving! So many of our troubles and worries come from not being satisfied with what we have. God has placed you where you are for His purpose so rejoice where you are! Be content with what you have, for it all comes from God. Trust God to take care of your needs and enjoy the freedom that comes with having God tell you that He will be there to help you. Trust Him to provide you with the important thing in life, salvation. Focus on His promise and stop worrying about worldly matters.

Hallelujah!!! Live with passion for the Lord. You should fear nothing and trust in Him. Man cannot destroy your eternal life. It is a gift to you from God. You are rich with the promises of God, so live life unafraid of the troubles of this world. He will not fail you…He will not desert you.

*"The fear of God leads to life,
a man has food and shelter, and no evil to fear."*

PROVERBS 19:23

HE HOLDS ALL THINGS

> *"For in Him were created all things in heaven and on earth: Thrones, Dominations, Sovereignties, Powers—all things were created through Him and for Him. Before anything was created He existed, and He holds all things in unity."*
>
> COLOSSIANS 1:16-17

Each of us is a creation of God. He knits us together and binds us in His love. We exist from His love, for His purpose, and we need to trust in Him that whatever happens to us is for His ultimate satisfaction. God is our God in the moment. Apart from the appreciation of His majesty we can never find contentment in what we have. We are where we are for a purpose, even though we may not see it. We have what we have for a purpose, even though we often forget to give thanks for it. We experience what we experience for a purpose, even though we may struggle to see the reasons at the time. He holds us together in times of praise and in times of trouble. God is intimately a part of everything you do, every experience you have, and every thought you have. He holds you together.

Some might think life is a progression of random acts that have no purpose. Others might believe we depend more upon luck than seeing God in everything. We complain and regret, failing to see the higher purpose and outcome that is to come. We blame God, or forget God, or push Him away in our shortsightedness. But He holds us together, even in our doubt. Contentment can only come when we trust that God is our God of every moment and that His love for each of us never fails. Faith requires that we trust God enough to still find joy in our challenges and peace in our circumstances. It takes effort to see God in everything and to keep our hearts in a condition of openness to Him. We may not always see it, but we need to trust that God is in complete control and He cares for His creation always, in every moment. Let the influence of frustration and lack of patience fall away when we know there is purpose in everything. His purpose. We should cast anxiousness and worry aside because we know ours is a God who never fails. Stay focused on how God can work in whatever circumstance we find ourselves because we know He holds us together in every moment and for eternity.

> *"Plans multiply in the human heart,*
> *But the purpose of God stands firm."*
>
> PROVERBS 19:21

FRUIT

"For every tree can be told by its own fruit…"

LUKE 6:44

A fruit tree cannot determine what kind of fruit it bears. You know the tree by its fruit. The fruit is the evidence of what kind of tree it is, as well as the condition of that tree. Can it bear no fruit? Is the fruit diseased? Is there plenty ripe for the plucking? What kind of fruit are you bearing? What kind of tree are you?

When Jesus is talking in this parable, He is using a simple image to describe the condition of the heart in all of man. If we are rooted in Jesus, nurtured by the watering of the Holy Spirit, it should be evident by the fruit that we bear. All those around us should be able to see our love, patience, and joy and realize that we are a "Jesus Tree." Our gentleness and compassion serve to reveal the One in whom we are rooted. Our fruits will be the natural results of a life committed, founded upon, and trusting in Jesus. Above all, being a "Jesus Tree" will bear the gift of love.

This verse is about hypocrisy. Jesus was telling us that we cannot claim to be a follower of Christ and continue to live as we did before becoming a Christian. We are called as Christians to actively display our fruit, letting our actions speak volumes about our commitment to Him. A tree bearing love cannot display hate. A tree bearing compassion cannot be selfish. A tree bearing humility cannot demand honor. A tree bearing peace cannot look for conflict. What kind of tree are you?

This verse is about integrity. Our actions directly show what is really going on in our hearts. They cannot be separated. Integrity is essential to bear fruit abundantly. When we strive to reveal our faith in God by being trustworthy, reliable, and committed, people can see what kind of tree we are. When we strive to do what is right in all circumstances, we bear the fruit of Spirit. When we speak truth and show patience and humbleness, we are showing that we belong to Christ. When we love, we reveal a Creator who first loved us.

This verse is about action. It is not enough to know or think about all the wonderful traits of Jesus. The expectation is that we put these traits into action. We should be different! What you do makes a difference! A "Jesus Tree" stands out by what it bears. We can be the living fruit of God's goodness. Let your fruit of the spirit thrive and be abundant!!

> *"From fruits of virtue grows a tree of life;*
> *The wicked are carried off before their time."*
>
> PROVERBS 11:30

PSALM 9

Verses 9-10

Verses 17-18

"May God be a stronghold for the oppressed,
A stronghold when times are hard.
Those who acknowledge Your name can rely on You,
You never desert those who seek You, God."

"God, You listen to the wants of the humble,
You bring strength to their hearts, You grant them a hearing,
Judging in favor of the orphaned and exploited,
So that earthborn man may strike fear no longer."

MY FOCUS

IN THE MEANTIME

> *"In the meantime, brothers, we wish you happiness;*
> *try to grow perfect; help one another. Be united; live in peace,*
> *and the God of love and peace will be with you."*

2 CORINTHIANS 13:11

In a world that seems to be getting angrier and angrier, what are we to do until Christ comes again? Exist in the happiness of Jesus. What are we to do when the flaws of a sinful world seem to have us surrounded? Grow toward perfection in Christ. How are we to survive at a time when selfishness and a "me first" attitude prevade our society? Help one another with a sacrificial, compassionate heart. At a time when racial and ethnic divides are becoming more pronounced, how can we be peacemakers? Be united with everyone in the Spirit of Christ. How do we thrive when anxiety and pressures seem to be mounting on us by the day? Let the peace of God that passes all understanding comfort you and give your rest.

In the meantime, we are called to persevere through troubled times as we trust the power and wisdom of God. In the meantime, we are called to stay faithful, trusting the absolute truth of God and in His promises. In the meantime, we are called to stand firm, never letting go of our desire to do what is right in the eyes of God. In the meantime, we are called to peace and rest because God has chosen to love us and have mercy on us. We can wait patiently and believe.

There are many times when we grow impatient and question why God does not act on our timetable. One absolute truth we can rely on is that God's timing is always perfect. Faith in God means that you trust His timing, His purposes, and His love. Our job, in the meantime, is to remain a child of God and put His love into action in our lives. Grow. Help. Unite. His love and peace are always close at hand, always within reach. Let your life reflect the happiness we can experience when we let God be the God of our lives.

> *"Then you will understand what virtue is, justice, and fair dealing, all paths that lead to happiness."*
>
> PROVERBS 2:9

GOD OF PEACE

"...since God is not a God of disorder but of peace."

1 CORINTHIANS 14:33

In a world that constantly struggles to find peace, we need God more than ever. When our lives are full of chaos and conflict, we need God more than ever. When we see strife and anger, we need God more than ever. At a time when disorder, hostility, and differences define us, we need God more than ever. The good news is He is always there, and He is a God of peace. Will you let Him be your God?

In being a follower of Jesus, it is essential that we be an example of peace in a hectic world. We can refuse to let our actions and attitudes be overtaken by what surrounds us and instead rely on Him for peace. We can turn our backs on division and separations as we look toward God to be the unifying source of true peace. We can set disappointment and guilt in their place when we live for a God whose promises are true and always in our best interest. In our times of disunity, He can unify. In our times of conflict, He can provide us with understanding and compassion. In our times of uneasiness, He can be the source of true peace, love, and grace. Will you let Him be your God?

The fear of what we don't know always leads to disorder and discomfort. In God, we know what our future is…eternity with Him at peace. In Him, there is no fear, no anxiety, and no worry. We live at a time when disorder seems to be all around us as we focus on differences rather than what unites us. God is the great unifier, the great rest to our soul, and the power that provides us with joy and hope. A world, a society, and we as individuals suffer when we lose sight of God. Without God, there is no peace. With God, there is peace that goes beyond what we could ever imagine. In Him, is rest, comfort, and assurance. In Him, is joy, hope, and contentment. When we cry out for peace we must remember that the source of peace, God, is right in front of us. When we look for solutions to the discord and disorder around us, we must remember that the source of harmony and peace, God, is right in front of us. He is peace. Will you let Him be your God?

"Do not say, 'I will repay evil';
Put your hope in God and He will keep you safe."

PROVERBS 20:22

FLEE FROM IDOLATRY

"Therefore, my dear friends, flee from idolatry."

1 CORINTHIANS 10:14

Have you ever stopped to think during the day what it is that you put your trust in? Is God the primary focus or do we turn our thoughts to our own "idols?" What is your idol? What was your focus yesterday? Did you put your faith in your own abilities, your social position, your pursuit of money? How many decisions were based on furthering the kingdom of God instead of furthering yourself? Indeed, we do have idols.

This verse does not tell us to accept idolatry or be tolerant of them. It directs us to flee from our idols, to distance ourselves as much as possible from them.

First, we need to take an accounting of each of our own idols. They come in so many forms. We worship many things throughout the day. We need to evaluate where we place our efforts and our hearts. Once we recognize them, our next job is to flee. It's not just stepping aside or stepping away. We are to flee! This may mean a drastic, active effort to change some things in our lives that are hard to change.

We have allowed so many things to replace God in our lives and have found ways to rationalize our misguided allegiances. Whatever in your life replaces God as your primary focus should be fled from. We must find priority in our life. We have been blessed with many things, but we have to realize where these gifts come from. We cannot honor the gifts, but instead honor the giver.

Dear Lord, help us to recognize and reconsider our focus and our priorities. Give us the wisdom, the ability, and the humility to put You first in our lives. Help us to flee from our idols.

*"Trust wholeheartedly in God,
put no faith in your own perception."*

PROVERBS 3:5

CELEBRATE

*"Afterwards he took them home and gave them a meal,
and the whole family celebrated their conversion to belief in God."*

ACTS 16:34

Celebrate! Be excited! Be thankful! Through faith, you are the sons and daughters of the Almighty God. Celebrate this and be excited! Through faith, you are righteous by the grace of the Almighty God. Be excited! Through faith, you WILL spend your eternity in the presence of the Almighty God. Be thankful!

It is so easy to forget what an awesome gift we have in Jesus. Day after day goes by with its worries zapping our enthusiasm for what is really important, the grace of God and the victory of Christ. There should be lightness about our living and an infectious joy in our character. There should be a smile on our face as we embrace the love that God reveals to us each and every day. There should be celebration in our hearts knowing that we are saved souls, getting to call ourselves children of God. Every day is a day for joy and celebration. Every day is a day for thankfulness and humility. Every day is a day to give glory and praise to our Father.

When we look at our daily lives we need to see how much of our time is spent worrying versus celebrating. Is our day consumed with negativity, overshadowing and pushing aside happiness? Do we let the negative news of the day replace the positives of a life lived with Christ? Do we let our anxieties overpower our real blessings? Knowing the love of God is reason to celebrate now and always.

It is time to spend more time smiling than frowning, more positive than negative, and more thankful than wanting. It is time to enjoy a real, intimate relationship with God and live with confidence in His grace. It is time for your routine to be one of celebration. Be known as someone who shows their thankfulness and happiness in the Lord for all to see. What a joy to be able to live as a forgiven sinner and a child of God. Be happy. Always. Let your life be one of celebration.

> *"He who listens closely to the Word shall find happiness;*
> *He who puts his trust in God is blessed."*
>
> PROVERBS 16:20

CHEERFUL HOPE

*"If you have hope, this will make you cheerful.
Do not give up if trials come; and keep on praying."*

ROMANS 12:12

Isn't it refreshing to be around someone who is constantly cheerful? They can change your mood in an instant with their upbeat attitude. They face the same obstacles, yet somehow find a way to stay cheerful through it all. They face hardships in their lives, but you would never know it as they let happiness and optimism overshadow fear and guilt. They are a breath of fresh air. That kind of attitude is not possible without hope. Do you need an attitude adjustment? Find hope in Jesus and let it rule your life.

Prayer is a powerful privilege given to all believers. There is nothing in our lives that cannot be brought to God in prayer. Prayer puts problems into perspective as we confess, thank, and ask our Father. With God on our side, how can we lose sight of the hope in His forgiveness? With God on our side, how can we let daily challenges overshadow the love of God? Light conquers darkness, hope conquers despair, and forgiveness conquers guilt.

Too often we give power to problems and forget the strength and perseverance that resides inside of us with hope in Him. We let worry and anxiousness take place over peace and rest. We allow doubt and negativity to overshadow promise and joy. But we have the best of all things on our side, God. We have true love and mercy on our side, God. We have a patient creator and an understanding father, God. Never give up and never give in to what steals your joy. We have what will always win inside of us, all the time, and in all circumstances. Take refuge in the hope of our Almighty God.

Smile more. Be cheerful. Be the refreshing spirit of God as you find hope in Him at all times. It will feel good.

> *"The hope of virtuous men is all joy,*
> *The expectations of the wicked are frustrated."*

PROVERBS 10:28

FREEDOM

"And in him, we gain our freedom, the forgiveness of our sins."

COLOSSIANS 1:14

Freedom comes with a price. That price was paid by Jesus. We are no longer defined by or restricted by sin. Jesus released us.

Freedom in Jesus allows us to honor God and love others. There are no boundaries to the love of God.

What makes God who He is? It is His love. Even though we sin, we know that we are forgiven through faith and His grace. Only God can provide that assurance. Christ has purchased our redemption with His blood. He paid for our sin, all of our sin, and has done away with it completely. Our sinful nature cannot get in the way of the power of His grace. The breadth and depth of His love can never be diminished by our failures. God is greater than that!

There is freedom in not having to hide part of ourselves from God. There is freedom in trusting God for salvation instead of trying to be good enough to experience Him. There is freedom to love others abundantly because we know God loves us in spite of our failures. In Him there is no guilt, balance due, or debt left unpaid. He paid it all, completely, for me and for you.

The gift of freedom is ours when we believe, trust, and rely on His grace. We will be free to witness and mirror love in all circumstances, understand and show empathy to those in need, and forgive and nurture others. We can live unrestricted and unmoved by sin as we let the love of Christ fill our hearts. We can act with kindness, appreciation, and fairness to all of God's creation. Because we are forgiven we can forgive. We can let our motives be pure and our intentions be transparent. We can make doing right a priority and let God be our center, guide, and reason for what we do. In Him, as forgiven sinners, we are free to love.

> *"The fear of God leads to life,*
> *A man has food and shelter, and no evil to fear."*

PROVERBS 19:23

PSALM 95

Verses 1-5

"Come, let us praise God joyfully,
Acclaiming the Rock of our safety;
Let us come into His presence with thanksgiving,
Acclaiming Him with music.
For God is a great God,
A greater King than all other gods;
From depths of earth to mountain top everything comes under His rule;
The sea belongs to Him, He made it,
So does the land, He shaped this too."

MY FOCUS

BELIEF IS A WORD OF ACTION

"You see now that it is by doing something good, and not only by believing, that a man is justified."

JAMES 2:24

Believing is not passive. A life built on believing in the saving grace of Christ is a life that produces the fruit of the Spirit. The reality of our faith is witnessed in the purpose and integrity of what we do. A belief that is never put into action does not honor Christ. What you do says a lot about what you believe and in whom you believe.

We can believe in a lot of things, but there is only one thing that can make an eternal difference: faith in Jesus Christ. We can accumulate knowledge about a lot of things, but we need one thing to turn that knowledge into a relationship: faith in Jesus Christ. We can dedicate our attention to a lot of things, but only one thing has the power to justify us: faith in Jesus Christ!

Be aware of what dominates what you believe in and how that belief affects your life. Doing good is the result of believing in something good. When we are saved through faith, we live in faith, actively putting into action the trust we have in Christ. We love because we believe. We forgive because we believe. We give thanks because we believe. We obey because we believe. The way we lead our lives reveals our faith in His grace.

Our belief in Christ and His saving grace has set us free to live a life full of the liberty and love that He provides. Our motives are God-driven. Our generosity reflects His gifts. Our peace comes from His righteousness. Our ability to do something good is our way of honoring and obeying a heavenly Father who never stops loving us. The fullness of our relationship to God goes beyond just believing to include a surrendered life dedicated to doing what is good and right. We do what we do because we serve a powerful, loving God. We do what we do as a response to a just, merciful God. We do what we do because we believe in His grace. Let your life be one of godly action, always declaring the Almighty God.

> *"To act virtuously and with justice*
> *Is more pleasing to God than sacrifice."*
>
> PROVERBS 21:3

FOCUS

*"The lamp of your body is your eye.
When your eye is sound, your whole body too is filled with light;
but when it is diseased your body too will be all darkness."*

LUKE 11:34

What you see influences you. Societal images are flying at us at an alarming pace, flooding us with image after image of what the world finds important. Television, movies, magazines, and computers bombard us with visual experiences. It is very difficult to not find some kind of violent or sexual image coming at us. It is easy to feel submerged by those impacts as they overwhelm our senses. Our brains crave more and more action, requiring us to multitask and soak in the images. What we see stimulates feeling and emotion, pulling us into identifying with the message. Just imagine how different we would feel if we had more spiritual images brought before us rather than images of the world. What we see can soften our hearts toward love or harden our hearts toward selfish gratification. What you see matters.

How you see. It is amazing how two people can look at the same image and see two very different things. We all see things with our own preconceived ideas, oftentimes seeing what we want to see instead of reality. We too often mold our vision to suit our preferred outcomes. We fail to see broader points of view, letting our prejudices and self-serving interests overcome our sense of sight. Fairness and truth become victims to ego and rationalization when we see only on our own terms. We also can be shortsighted, wanting instant results without seeing the future consequences. How you see matters.

Focus. Through what lens should we look? Focus your sight through compassion, truth, and love. These are the real, tangible outcomes when we look at everything through the lens of Christ. Focusing first and foremost on Him, we can search to see the good, the honesty, and the power of forgiveness in the world around us. By focusing on Christ we can fill our entire being with light. He can make our hearts whole and our bodies shine as we live focused on Him. The more we see Christ in everything, the more the whole body can be used to provide more light to a world in need. Be healthy in heart and soul, letting Christ be the focus of your eye and the focus of your life. See the good, find the best, build up, and commit to Christ. May we all focus on Christ and let everything enter our eyes through the lens of His peace and love. Be filled with the light.

> *"The light of virtuous men burns bright,*
> *The lamp of the wicked goes out."*
>
> **PROVERBS 13:9**

FAITH IN WHAT?

"Through Him you now have faith in God, who raised Him from the dead and gave Him glory for that very reason—so that you would have faith and hope in God."

1 PETER 1:21

In our pursuit of safety and peace, we look many different places and put our faith in many different things to make them come true. When we feel that there is part of us missing, we look everywhere to feel complete and important. When we want more, we look everywhere to try to find happiness and contentment. Yet apart from God, we never find what satisfies us.

We trust technology, but sometimes struggle to send an email. We trust doctors, but they cannot heal a broken heart. We trust in the government, but passing laws will not change a heart uninterested in change. We trust in money, but we never seem to have enough of it. We trust in power, but power eventually runs out. We trust in our friends, but find it hard to give forgiveness when they fail us. Apart from God, we come up empty time after time.

There is only one thing that deserves our unwavering and complete trust, God. We do not need to put our hope in things, we need to put our faith in God. When everything disappoints us, we need to refocus on where our real hope is, God. Why do we have the Bible? So that we may believe. Why did Christ suffer and die for us? So that we may be forgiven. Why was Christ raised from the dead? So that we may find life with Him. Why does Christ now reign eternal in heaven? So that we can experience the totality of His love. Why is the Spirit active in our lives? Without the Spirit, we would never experience the power, wisdom, and love of God first hand. Through Christ, we are blessed to have both faith and hope in the only person that will never fail, God. Put your faith in what really matters.

"Trust wholeheartedly in God,
Put no faith in your own perception."

PROVERBS 3:5

ENDURE YOUR HARDSHIPS

"Endure hardship as discipline; God is treating you as sons."

HEBREWS 12:7

What kind of father would God be if He did not discipline you? All children need discipline in order to grow and mature. Thank God for His discipline!

Learn from the difficulties that are put before you today. How do you demonstrate your trust and faith in God in the face of adversity? It is easy to be faithful when everything is going well, but the depth of your faith is shown when you are challenged. How will you react when your storm comes? Is your faith strong enough that you stay in the heart of God and treat the situation according to His will? Or do you need more maturity? Every experience you have should be used to strengthen your faith.

Notice this verse says to endure. It does not say change the hardship or avoid it. It implies that we are to accept the challenges put before us and use these experiences to solidify our trust and dependence on God. This means to be patient in your hardship, remaining grounded in your hope, and realizing that there is a purpose.

God is teaching you lessons today. Every event reveals your weakness. It becomes evident that we need to trust God, for He can give you the power to endure. As you persist with Jesus, you learn how to trust, to hope, and to remain humble. Examine the lessons learned during your hardships and endure. God is your Father. He has you.

> *"He who spurns his father's discipline is a fool,*
> *he who accepts correction is discreet."*

PROVERBS 15:5

FAITH IS YOUR GUARANTEE

*"Only faith can guarantee the blessings that we hope for,
or prove the existence of the realities that at present remain unseen."*

HEBREWS 11:1

Faith is real. You can see it demonstrated in people's lives. You can see the way it affects the way believers live. It gives your life purpose.

Hope is real. There is no hope or faith without a soul. God's promises fill our soul, and our faith guarantees that these promises are true. Faith is knowing that promises are reality. God touches us inexplicably. To the unbeliever, faith is an abstract thought, one that cannot be proven or reasoned. But to the believer, faith is very real and lives within us. It determines who we are, why we live, and how we live. Our faith gives us purpose and quality.

Let your faith expand. Allow it to grow deeper. Allow it to transform you into what God wants you to be. Faith is spiritual. Faith is a blessing. Are you sure of the promises of God? Are you certain of what you cannot see? Be fertile soil for your faith to mature and grow. Does your life reveal the depth of your conviction? Does your life reveal the degree of your trust?

Pray that your faith continues to grow. Feed your faith daily and trust in God. Depend on the promises of God, and live in the knowledge that the unseen is real. Let God live within you today and always.

FOCUS

*"Man's spirit is the lamp of God,
searching his deepest self."*

PROVERBS 20:27

FAITH EQUALS HAPPINESS

"...and happy is the man who does not lose faith in Me."

LUKE 7:23

How do you define happiness? In what or in whom do you put your faith? Above all else, what do you value? See if the following definition represents the type of relationship you have with Christ.

Faith: firm belief in the reliability, truth, ability, or strength of someone or something. "Relations have to be built on trust."

These descriptions of a firm belief describe God perfectly.

Reliable: While everything we see around us fails, God is reliable. Only He is the same today, yesterday, and tomorrow. He never changes His mind or commitment to us personally and universally. He is never far away.

Truth: We now live in a world that struggles with truth. Truth has become subjective and an ever-changing target. Too many people in this age of misinformation and propaganda constantly try to mold truth for their own purposes, desperately trying to convert others to their points of view and perceptions. God, on the other hand, is the perfect truth. He never changes, cannot be corrupted, and never fails.

Able: Too often we look to outside entities to solve our problems, relying on others to mold our futures. There is only one source of wisdom and power that has the true ability to provide for all of us here and in eternity. He alone has the power. He alone has the majesty. He alone has the ability. It is time to stop looking at others or ourselves and turn back to God.

Strong: Too often we feel powerless. We feel like we cannot control any parts of our lives, despite trying and trying. There is no doubt that we all have our weaknesses, and those weaknesses show themselves over and over again. Without God, we do not and cannot succeed for eternity.

Relationship: Lasting relationships have to be built on trust. Do you trust God? Do you trust Him enough to bring yourself to a point where you FIRMLY believe? Real contentment, independent of circumstances, is available to all of us through faith in God. All other things may fail, but God meets the definition of faith.

God is at His best when we are at our weakest. When we realize that He and He alone is worthy of our faith, we are at our best. Let God lift your everyday burden as we live a life focused on the reliability, strength, ability, and truth of God. Turn your frustration, sadness, and anxiousness into hope, surety, and joy through faith in God. We have choices to make as we decide the object of our faith. May we all choose God.

> *"Trust wholeheartedly in God,*
> *Put no faith in your own perception."*
>
> **PROVERBS 3:5**

PSALM 104

Verses 19-23

"You made the moon to tell the seasons,
The sun knows when to set:
You bring darkness on, night falls, all the forest animals come out:
Savage lions roaring for their prey, claiming their food from God.
The sun rises, they retire,
Going back to lie down in their lairs, and man goes out to work,
And to labor until dusk.
God, what variety You have created,
Arranging everything so wisely!
Earth is completely full of things You have made."

MY FOCUS

GOOD WORKS BELONG TO GOD

*"Be careful not to parade your good deeds before men
to attract their notice; by doing this you will lose all reward
from your Father in heaven."*

MATTHEW 6:1

Good deeds are an expression of obedience, love, and honor to God. Anytime self-promotion becomes part of the reason for our good deeds, we have missed the point entirely. Good deeds are nothing more than the visible result of our commitment to God and His children. Good deeds allow God to be visible on earth as He uses us to reach out to those around us. Through us, God can display His goodness and glory.

Who put the desire inside us to do good works? God did. Who opens our eyes and hearts to be aware of the needs of others? God does. Who gives us the capacity and unselfish heart to carry out His good works? God does. The good deeds of God do not have an ulterior motive. The foundation of good works can be found in humility and sacrifice. The welfare of others comes before our own ambitions.

Do not make the mistake of thinking you actually own what you have. Every possession you have is on loan to you from God. Our job on earth is to be good stewards of the gifts that God has loaned to us for His purposes. As God's agents we strive to do good works, not for attention or advantage for ourselves, but to witness to the world the power, strength, and goodness of God. God is the center of all good works. Through our commitment and obedience to God, we can be used as a distribution method of God's good deeds.

Motives tell much about a person's relationship with God. Why do you do what you do? Examine your motives on a daily basis to determine if humility and servanthood rather than pride and self-edification are the driving forces of your actions. Will your motivations reveal your personal relationship with God, or your degree of separation? Let God be glorified in all that you do.

"Pride comes first, disgrace comes after;
With the humble is wisdom found."

PROVERBS 11:2

DO YOU WANT TO BE WELL?

"...and when Jesus saw him lying there and knew
he had been in this condition for a long time,
He said, 'Do you want to be well again?'"

JOHN 5:6

Too often our attention is taken up by what we want instead of what we have. We all suffer from an infirmity, whether it is physical, mental, or spiritual. We get caught up looking at what we don't have instead of celebrating our abundance in Him. We carry guilt and pain with us as baggage, letting it weigh us down and keep us from the peace and healing found in Jesus.

The person to whom Jesus asked this question had been lying by the pool of healing for thirty-eight years, waiting for someone to carry him to the water. He waited and waited, blaming others for taking his turn for a miracle. It's a fair question to ask him: how badly do you want to be healed? How long will you sit at the water's edge until you find a way to Jesus? We complain but look to ourselves instead of Jesus for peace. We harden our hearts, forgetting that it is up to us to seek Jesus. We blame others, failing to take responsibility for our own relationship with Him. What do you really want?

Shortly after this verse Jesus miraculously heals this man, releasing him from the barriers to his faith. How many barriers do we put in the way of letting God be God? How long will we wait to be healed by faith in Him? How long will we let our own limitations get in the way of reliance on Jesus? Do you want to be well again?

The power of Jesus was greater than any infirmity, any limitation, and any excuse. The healed man immediately took up his mat and walked. He was set free by the power of Jesus. Do you want that power to be a force in your life? Do you want to see freedom or stay in bondage? Do you want to rest in His magnificent power or rely on yourself? Do you want to let His grace and glory change your life or will you be satisfied to let your life stay muddled in its present state? The source of healing and growth is Jesus. The strength to thrive is available to us through Him. He is stronger than anything that holds us back from an abundant life centered in Him.

What do you want? Do you want to be well again? Jesus is always there, waiting for your answer.

"When a man has a ready answer he has joy too:
How satisfying is the apt reply."

PROVERBS 4:23

HIS PEACE

"Peace I bequeath to you, My own peace I give you,
a peace the world cannot give, this is My gift to you.
Do not let your hearts be troubled or afraid."

JOHN 14:27

It seems like the world is becoming undone, yet we look in the wrong direction for peace. People are angry and quick to judge, yet we fail to see our own failings. People look for power and advantage over the weak, yet do not recognize their own weakness. People condemn and judge without seeing their own sin. We, as individuals and as a world, need God more than ever. Still we labor on, trying to do things our own way, pushing God aside. It is time we looked in the right place. God has a gift of peace for us: His presence.

Day after day we are bombarded with images of a world in turmoil. Fear and worry can so easily overtake us as we see things crumble around us. The level of anxiety in our society seems to be escalating as we feel threatened. We search and yearn for peace, but forget that the gift of peace has already been given to us. Whatever goes on around us, the presence of God in our heart is the source of true peace. A gift. His gift to us. Peace. The presence of God.

The peace that passes all understanding has been given to us, bequeathed, because we are heirs with Christ. We do not need to overcome the world, He already has. We do not need to live a life in fear or in anxiousness because His peace is greater than what the world can ever offer. His presence is powerful. His presence is spiritual rest. His presence is a life lived freely in the confidence of our creator. Think outside of this world and into God. Faith in the world fails. Faith in God gives peace.

Without the presence of God, no matter what you have you will never find real peace. More money, a better job, a new political leader, a new law, or a new neighbor is not the answer to your search for peace. The world cannot protect you from fear. God can. The world does not have a solution to your anxiety. God does. The world cannot ease your worries. God can. The world battles for your mind, but God has already won your heart and soul, paying the price for you. God is victorious for you. There is peace in that victory, His victory for you.

Search out God in every situation. Feel His presence and grab hold of His peace. God has you covered in His grace. Rest in His victory and His power. Enjoy real, true, meaningful, lasting peace. The presence of God.

"Better a dry crust and with it peace,
than a house where feast and dispute go together."

PROVERBS 17:1

CHOOSE TO LOVE

"We are to love, then, because He loved us first."

1 JOHN 4:19

God's affection for us gives us both the freedom to love and the obligation to love Him and our neighbors. The essence of God is love, and with His love in us, we should reflect that love to others. God's love is so immense and so complete that we, through faith, are led by it to an abundant life of love. We are obligated. We have the capacity. We must.

Unlike God, too often we are stingy with our love. We pick and choose who we think is worthy of our time and emotion, selfishly holding back our love. Too often we set a criteria and expectation before we love. Can you love someone exactly as they are, or is your love dependent upon your perceptions? God loves us as we are. Can you love someone even though they have disappointed you? God loves us despite our continuing failures. Each one of us is a specifically created person who is loved by God. God is love. God always loves. God loved first. As we respond to the love of God, we should remember how intense, active, and complete His love is for each of us. His love is sacrificial, all inclusive, and powerful. His love is sufficient, abundant, and pure. His love is trustworthy, real, and passionate. His love is patient, overflowing, and present. Love is the character and essence of God.

Can you let this kind of love become part of your character? How will you respond to that kind of love?

His love can bring peace, joy, and satisfaction. Can we bring that kind of response into each moment of the day? When we see a need, do we meet it out of our respect for the love of God? Do we hesitate, compromise, or look the other way, or do we respond in love? God's love shows no boundaries. What is stopping you from showing the same kind of love? God's kind of love is the opposite of fear. We can live assured of His love, power and grace. Through faith in our loving God, we are free to respond in love at all times for one simple reason. He loved us first.

> *"Let love and faithfulness never leave you; Bind them around your neck, write them on the tablet of your heart."*
>
> **PROVERBS 3:3 NIV**

AS I HAVE LOVED YOU

"This is My commandment: love one another, as I have loved you."

JOHN 15:12

Love is not an option to be used at our own discretion. Love is not a tool we use when we need something in return. Love is a commandment. Love is the outward proof that we belong to Christ. Love frames our attitudes, actions, and perceptions. Love like you belong to Christ.

Imagine what this world would be like if we all followed this commandment. Imagine if every conversation revolved around compassion, understanding, and empathy. Imagine if every response considered the betterment of others and the wisdom in each word. Imagine people willingly sacrificing for others in an attitude of peace. Imagine looking for the best in others rather than reasons to divide. Imagine listening and understanding being the primary goals of a relationship. Imagine a spirit of unity, putting aside differences for the good of God's purposes. Imagine striving for equality, because God loves us all equally. Imagine loving as a way of life and a means to honor and identify with our creator, atoner, justifier, and advocate. Imagine being used by God as a messenger in His grace.

However, imagination is not what Christ commands. This command is about action. It is about a continual, overarching character of care and compassion. It requires purposeful thought to see the events and interactions of our life through the lens of Christ. Love will change our outlook and actions in a real, tangible way.

So what do we have to do to love "as I have loved you?" How did He love?

Obediently. Christ loved so much that He obediently gave His life to save each one of us.

Sacrificially. He was willing to take on the sins of each of us, to let us live free.

Completely. His love is unconditional, seeing everyone as an individual created in the image of God.

Gracefully. His love does not depend on us…it originates in Him.

Compassionately. He knows us, our fears, our sins, our motives.

Selflessly. He was the ultimate sacrifice giving the ultimate evidence of the fullness of His love

Can we love like Christ? Yes, through and in Christ. Let His love overpower the anger, resentment, and disrespect that surrounds us. Let His love empower each of us to prioritize others above self, understanding over prejudice, and love over all. Love intentionally. Love fully. Love knowing He loves us.

"Hatred provokes disputes,
Love covers over all offences."

PROVERBS 10:12

FOUNDED ON THE ROCK

"Rain came down, floods rose, gales blew and hurled themselves against the house, and it did not fall; it was founded on the rock."

MATTHEW 7:25

The storms of life can come at us very quickly with the potential for plenty of damage. It is all too common to feel the forces against us batter us until we feel overwhelmed and unable to cope. Keeping our heads above water during times in our lives that challenge us can be quite a task. It is easy to get swept away if we do not have a strong foundation. That foundation, that rock, is Jesus.

When the storms come, we look for safety and comfort. When we feel swept away by the tides of calamity and discord, we look for something steady and sure to hang on to. When we feel the forces of trials and troubles blow us around, we look for focus and a straight path to follow. When we feel pressured from the outside and are challenged to remain faithful, we look for what we know is true, trustworthy, and genuine. What we need to look for is Jesus. Hold on. Hold tight. Rest in His arms.

Jesus is our rock. He never fails and is not overtaken by rain, flood, or winds. He stands firm, solid, and unchanged. Grabbing hold of Him, we can withstand the onslaught of sin in our lives, knowing that our foundation and future is secure. With Him, we cannot be swept away. With Him, our house stands up to every danger from the outside. With Him, the winds of outside influences cannot take us off His path and away from His grace. With Him, we can be sure, content, and confident even in the worst of storms.

Hold on to the rock of Jesus and let Him hold on to you. It is His grace and love that is worthy to be held on to tightly just as we are valued by Him as He embraces us. We are connected to Jesus, the rock, through our faith and His grace. Never let go.

"By wisdom, God set the earth on its foundations,
By discernment, He fixed the heavens firm."

PROVERBS 3:19

PERSON OF PEACE

"May the Lord of peace Himself give you peace all the time and in every way. The Lord will be with you all."

2 THESSALONIANS 3:18

I have to admit that I am constantly looking for peace in the wrong places. I long for a quiet place that lets me relax and get away from it all. I try to isolate myself from all the things that are going wrong in the world. I want to stop being frustrated by the everyday challenges of life. I am looking for peace in circumstance, forgetting that peace can only really come from one source…the person of peace…Jesus.

We live in a world full of conflict, full of division, and full of pride. We are surrounded by negativity and sensationalism, frustration and demands. We let the noise of the world spoil our quiet and rest in Jesus. If we look for circumstances to give us peace we will never find it. Peace is a person. Jesus.

Want to find peace all the time? Faith in Jesus is the only way. Want to find peace in every way? Faith in Jesus is the only way. He is the Lord of peace, the giver of contentment, and the only source for true rest. He offers eternal peace, all the time, in every way. It is time we all start looking in the right place for peace, Jesus. We can see very clearly that the world will only ever offer temporary solutions and another crisis is right around the corner. But Jesus offers constant peace when we rely on Him, His promises, and His power. The world fails. Jesus never fails. The world constantly changes. Jesus remains unchanged. The demands of the world are never met. Believe in Jesus, and you share in His victory. Reject the weakness of peace in circumstance, and accept the power of the person of peace, Jesus.

> *"He who listens closely to the Word shall find happiness;*
> *He who puts his trust in God is blessed."*
>
> PROVERBS 16:20

PSALM 51

Verses 1-2
Verses 10-11
Verses 14-15

"Have mercy on me, O God, in Your goodness,
In Your great tenderness wipe away my faults;
Wash me clean of my guilt,
Purify me from my sin."

"God, create a clean heart in me,
Put into me a new and constant spirit,
Do not banish me from Your presence,
Do not deprive me of Your Holy Spirit."

"Save me from death, God my savior,
And my tongue will acclaim You righteousness;
Lord, open my lips,
And my mouth will speak out Your praise."

MY FOCUS

MY FOCUS

MY FOCUS

MY FOCUS

MY FOCUS